I0889038

TABLE OF CONTENTS

Top 15 Test Taking Tips

1. Know the test directions, duration, topics, question types, how many questions
2. Setup a flexible study schedule at least 3-4 weeks before test day
3. Study during the time of day you are most alert, relaxed, and stress free
4. Maximize your learning style; visual learner use visual study aids, auditory learner use auditory study aids
5. Focus on your weakest knowledge base
6. Find a study partner to review with and help clarify questions
7. Practice, practice, practice
8. Get a good night's sleep; don't try to cram the night before the test
9. Eat a well balanced meal
10. Wear comfortable, loose fitting, layered clothing; prepare for it to be either cold or hot during the test
11. Eliminate the obviously wrong answer choices, then guess the first remaining choice
12. Pace yourself; don't rush, but keep working and move on if you get stuck
13. Maintain a positive attitude even if the test is going poorly
14. Keep your first answer unless you are positive it is wrong
15. Check your work, don't make a careless mistake

Chapter 1 - Place Value and Number Sense

Lesson 1

Place Value 1-100,000

The place value of a digit is determined by where it is in a number.

Hundred Thousands	Ten Thousands	Thousands	Hundreds	Tens	Ones
1	2	3	4	5	6

123,456

One Hundred Twenty Three Thousand, Four Hundred Fifty Six

Write these numbers correctly in the blanks.

1. 422,719 =

4	2	2	7	1	9
Hundred Thousands	Ten Thousands	Thousands	Hundreds	Tens	Ones

2. 982,124 =

Hundred Thousands	Ten Thousands	Thousands	Hundreds	Tens	Ones

3. 263,927 =

Hundred Thousands	Ten Thousands	Thousands	Hundreds	Tens	Ones

4. 627,141 =

Hundred Thousands	Ten Thousands	Thousands	Hundreds	Tens	Ones

5. 891,362 =

Hundred Thousands	Ten Thousands	Thousands	Hundreds	Tens	Ones

Place Value Big numbers 1-1,000,000

The place value of a digit is determined by where it is in a number.

Millions	Hundred Thousands	Ten Thousands	Thousands	Hundreds	Tens	Ones
1	2	3	4	5	6	7

1,234,567

One million, two hundred thirty-four thousand, five hundred sixty-seven

1. 6,138,462 =

6	1	3	8	4	6	2
Millions	Hundred Thousands	Ten Thousands	Thousands	Hundreds	Tens	Ones

2. 3,194,675 =

Millions	Hundred Thousands	Ten Thousands	Thousands	Hundreds	Tens	Ones

3. 8,417,205 =

Millions	Hundred Thousands	Ten Thousands	Thousands	Hundreds	Tens	Ones

4. 2,765,447 =

Millions	Hundred Thousands	Ten Thousands	Thousands	Hundreds	Tens	Ones

5. 5,925,057 =

Millions	Hundred Thousands	Ten Thousands	Thousands	Hundreds	Tens	Ones

Lesson 2

Identifying Place Value - Word Problems

Solve the word problems below.

1. In the number 25,483 :

A. This digit is in the one's place ________
B. This digit is in the hundred's place ________
C. The 5 is in the ______________ place
D. The 8 is in the ______________ place

2. In the number 62,134 :

A. This digit is in the ten's place ________
B. This digit is in the thousand's place ________
C. The 6 is in the ______________ place
D. The 4 is in the ______________ place

3. In the number 84,327 :

A. This digit is in the one's place ________
B. This digit is in the thousand's place ________
C. The 2 is in the ______________ place
D. The 8 is in the ______________ place

4. In the number 14,960 :

A. This digit is in the hudred's place ________
B. This digit is in the ten-thousand's place ________
C. The 0 is in the ______________ place
D. The 4 is in the ______________ place

5. In the number 40,589 :

A. This digit is in the one's place ________
B. This digit is in the hundred's place ________
C. The 0 is in the ______________ place
D. The 4 is in the ______________ place

Lesson 3

Rounding up to 10,000

Round the following numbers to the nearest hundred.

1. 891 900

2. 212 ________

3. 602 ________

4. 598 ________

5. 775 ________

6. 349 ________

7. 239 ________

8. 621 ________

9. 440 ________

10. 112 ________

Round the following numbers to the nearest thousand.

11. 9,054 ________

12. 3,567 ________

13. 2,969 ________

14. 6,056 ________

15. 7,476 ________

16. 2,113 ________

17. 8,631 ________

18. 5,589 ________

19. 1,551 ________

20. 4,999 ________

Round the following numbers to the nearest ten-thousand.

21. 49,508 ________

22. 72,497 ________

23. 12,023 ________

24. 51,515 ________

25. 88,720 ________

26. 42,023 ________

27. 20,653 ________

28. 13,749 ________

Rounding up to 100,000

Round the following numbers to the nearest thousand.

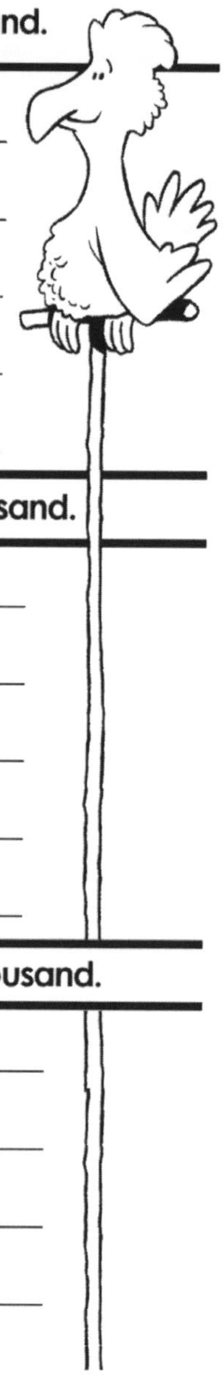

1. 2,563 ________

2. 9,198 ________

3. 1,423 ________

4. 7,712 ________

5. 3,300 ________

6. 4,219 ________

7. 5,756 ________

8. 8,154 ________

9. 6,069 ________

10 1,995 ________

Round the following numbers to the nearest ten-thousand.

11. 39,092 ________

12. 19,917 ________

13. 93,254 ________

14. 56,055 ________

15. 70,856 ________

16. 77,150 ________

17. 33,809 ________

18. 35,451 ________

19. 20,901 ________

20. 48,599 ________

Round the following numbers to the nearest hundred-thousand.

21. 274,333 ________

22. 596,559 ________

23. 221,324 ________

24. 530,708 ________

25. 189,365 ________

26. 317,110 ________

27. 882,658 ________

28. 610,567 ________

29. 789,381 ________

30. 109,277 ________

Lesson 4

Expanded Form

We learned earlier that every digit in a number has a place value. **Expanded form** shows that number expanded into an addition statement.

Example:

The expanded form of 5,786 is:
5,000 + 700 + 80 + 6.

Write each number in expanded form.

1. 82 — 80 + 2
2. 29 — ________
3. 56 — ________
4. 74 — ________
5. 35 — ________
6. 99 — ________
7. 250 — ________
8. 629 — ________
9. 150 — ________
10. 892 — ________
11. 905 — ________
12. 427 — ________

13. Twenty - Nine — 20 + 9
14. Seventy - One — ________
15. Eighty - Six — ________
16. Fifty - Four — ________
17. Sixteen — ________
18. Thirty - Eight — ________

Expanded Form 2

Write each number in expanded form.

1. 156 ______ **2.** 658 ______ **3.** 295 ______ **4.** 431 ______

5. 567 ______ **6.** 155 ______ **7.** 832 ______ **8.** 394 ______

9. 2,591 ______ **10.** 8,942 ______ **11.** 4,154 ______

12. 6,387 ______ **13.** 1,582 ______ **14.** 3,578 ______

15. 44,658 ______ **16.** 73,435 ______

17. 95,261 ______ **18.** 37,872 ______

Lesson 5

Ordering up to 10,000

Write these numbers in order from least to greatest.

1. 9,289 | 92,891 | 9,281 | 96,381 9,281 9,289 92,891 96,381
2. 23,112 | 23,111 | 22,311 | 2,313 __________
3. 7,856 | 7,855 | 78,855 | 78,856 __________
4. 11,112 | 1,111 | 11,131 | 10,112 __________
5. 4,326 | 44,326 | 44,436 | 4,316 __________
6. 3,289 | 3,891 | 3,819 | 3,818 __________
7. 57,289 | 57,891 | 57,211 | 57,500 __________
8. 60,255 | 6,552 | 66,252 | 6,255 __________
9. 15,247 | 15,250 | 15,248 | 15,249 __________
10. 9,564 | 92,564 | 9,546 | 93,564 __________
11. 8,219 | 84,921 | 84,218 | 84,219 __________

Ordering up to 100,000

Write these numbers in order from least to greatest.

1. 100,289 | 100,891 | 100,280 | 100,381 ____________________
2. 512,112 | 512,123 | 51,110 | 512,101 ____________________
3. 855,622 | 865,622 | 856,628 | 856,629 ____________________
4. 634,209 | 634,101 | 635,700 | 633,601 ____________________
5. 231,115 | 20,115 | 231,150 | 21,115 ____________________
6. 546,029 | 546,209 | 546,030 | 546,020 ____________________
7. 375,787 | 355,891 | 355,111 | 375,375 ____________________
8. 23,151 | 239,151 | 237,151 | 240,151 ____________________
9. 155,289 | 146,891 | 145,280 | 145,381 ____________________
10. 269,722 | 20,722 | 269,772 | 266,722 ____________________
11. 990,281 | 90,821 | 90,280 | 90,281 ____________________
12. 175,337 | 76,337 | 75,337 | 7,537 ____________________

Lesson 6

Number Patterns to 10,000

Complete the number patterns.

1. 10,475 | 10,485 | 10,495 | 11,005

2. 98,211 | ________ | ________ | 98,511

3. ________ | 62,001 | ________ | 64,001

4. 22,729 | 22,829 | ________ | ________

5. ________ | 82,657 | ________ | 84,657

6. 2,475 | 2,485 | ________ | ________

7. 11,303 | ________ | ________ | 14,303

8. ________ | 42,370 | ________ | 44,370

9. 72,112 | 72,119 | ________ | ________

10. 33,776 | ________ | ________ | 36,776

12. ________ | 79,061 | ________ | 99,061

Number Patterns to 100,000

Complete the number patterns.

1. 980,211 | ________ | ________ | 980,511

2. ________ | 621,001 | ________ | 619,001

3. 282,729 | 282,829 | ________ | ________

4. ________ | 694,657 | ________ | 694,677

5. 111,729 | 112,729 | ________ | ________

6. ________ | 350,001 | ________ | 352,001

7. 523,303 | ________ | ________ | 526,303

8. ________ | 815,370 | ________ | 825,370

9. ________ | 256,119 | 356,119 | ________

10. 609,776 | ________ | ________ | 639,776

11. 110,383 | 115,383 | ________ | ________

12. 340,303 | ________ | ________ | 370,303

Chapter 2 - Addition

Lesson 1

2-Digit Addition - Regrouping 1

To add multiple digit numbers together, start in the ones place and then use basic addition rules. When the number equals ten or more the first digit carries over to the next spot. This is called **regrouping**.

Step 1: Add the digits in the one's column.

	Hundred's	Ten's	One's
		8	5
+		1	7
			2

Step 2: Carry the 1 over to the top of the ten's column.

	Hundred's	Ten's	One's
		1	
		8	5
x		1	7
		1	2

Step 3: Add all the digits in the ten's column together.

	Hundred's	Ten's	One's
		1	
		+	
		8	5
		+	
x		1	7
	1	0	2

Solve the problems below.

1. 49 + 32 = 81	**2.** 58 + 7	**3.** 83 + 84	**4.** 42 + 9	**5.** 52 + 72
6. 44 + 5	**7.** 32 + 14	**8.** 18 + 20	**9.** 71 + 92	**10.** 59 + 6
11. 81 + 9	**12.** 60 + 57	**13.** 32 + 40	**14.** 19 + 2	**15.** 27 + 86

Lesson 2

2-Digit Addition - Regrouping 2

To add multiple digit numbers together, start in the ones place and then use basic addition rules. When the number equals ten or more the first digit carries over to the next spot. This is called **regrouping**.

Solve the problems below.

1. 78 + 14	**2.** 64 + 39	**3.** 79 + 99	**4.** 34 + 75	**5.** 49 + 29
6. 58 + 87	**7.** 15 + 46	**8.** 27 + 67	**9.** 70 + 49	**10.** 13 + 9
11. 35 + 68	**12.** 80 + 27	**13.** 48 + 24	**14.** 34 + 57	**15.** 55 + 37
16. 99 + 56	**17.** 68 + 68	**18.** 40 + 85	**19.** 74 + 66	**20.** 63 + 99

Lesson 3

2-Digit 3-Row Addition - Regrouping 1

To add multiple digit numbers together, start in the ones place and then use basic addition rules. When the number equals ten or more the first digit carries over to the next spot. This is called **regrouping**.

Solve the problems below.

1. 36 22 + 15	**2.** 84 70 + 9	**3.** 64 29 + 42	**4.** 57 52 + 73	**5.** 44 15 + 39
6. 66 99 + 82	**7.** 50 36 + 55	**8.** 15 35 + 80	**9.** 67 72 + 18	**10.** 11 28 + 37
11. 62 97 + 19	**12.** 55 20 + 12	**13.** 18 19 + 20	**14.** 22 76 + 8	**15.** 77 37 + 47
16. 46 44 + 56	**17.** 98 49 + 89	**18.** 75 57 + 6	**19.** 36 62 + 19	**20.** 99 95 + 92

2-Digit 3-Row Addition - Regrouping 2

To add multiple digit numbers together, start in the ones place and then use basic addition rules. When the number equals ten or more the first digit carries over to the next spot. This is called **regrouping**.

Solve the problems below.

1.	2.	3.	4.	5.
12	72	72	30	23
60	44	16	82	67
+ 42	+ 55	+ 11	+ 8	+ 94

6.	7.	8.	9.	10.
50	24	81	96	75
32	72	12	64	11
+ 86	+ 39	+ 4	+ 51	+ 70

11.	12.	13.	14.	15.
44	88	20	99	60
79	52	36	85	92
+ 93	+ 6	+ 24	+ 13	+ 41

16.	17.	18.	19.	20.
30	77	10	92	17
57	12	28	68	29
+ 94	+ 9	+ 96	+ 47	+ 3

Lesson 4

Addition Word Problems

Use addition to solve the problems below.

1. Elle picked apples for four days. On day one she picked 10 apples. On day two she picked 26 apples. On day three she picked 14 apples. On day four she picked 14 apples. How many apples does Elle have in total?

____

2. Cindy has been doing her chores every day after school. On Monday she swept the floor for 12 minutes. On Tuesday she spent 9 minutes making her bed. On Wednesday she washed the dishes for 20 minutes. On Thursday she spent 15 minutes vacuuming the floor. How much time did she spend on her chores?

____

3. Steven is good at basketball. In game one he scored 14 points. In game two he scored 22 points. In game three he scored 27. In games four and five he scored 17 and 12 points. How many points has Steven scored so far?

____

4. Amy loves to read, she reads every day after school. One day she read 45 minutes. The next day she read 30 minutes. The day after that she spent 57 minutes reading. Yesterday she read for 26 minutes and today she spent 15 minutes reading her book. How much time has she spent reading this week.

____

Lesson 5

3-Digit Addition - Regrouping 1

To add multiple-digit numbers together, start in the ones place and then use basic addition rules. When a number equals ten or more the first digit carries over to the next spot. This is called **regrouping**.

Step 1: Add the digits in the one's column and carry over the 1 to the ten's column.

	1000's	100's	10's	1's
			1	
		6	4	3
+		5	8	9
				2

Step 2: Next add the digits in the tens's column and carry over the 1 to the hundred's column.

	1000's	100's	10's	1's
		1	1	
		6	4	3
+		5	8	9
			3	2

Step 3: Next add the digits in the hundred's column.

	1000's	100's	10's	1's
		1	1	
		6	4	3
+		5	8	9
		2	3	2

Step 4: Finally, carry over the 1 from the hundred's column to the thousands's column.

	1000's	100's	10's	1's
		1	1	
		6	4	3
+		5	8	9
	1	2	3	2

Solve the problems below. Use regrouping when needed.

1. 498 + 321 = 819

2. 580 + 729

3. 134 + 22

4. 309 + 447

5. 253 + 203

6. 171 + 82

7. 344 + 493

8. 714 + 507

9. 629 + 78

10. 629 + 351

3-Digit Addition - Regrouping 2

Solve the problems below using regrouping.

1. 151 + 459	**2.** 239 + 205	**3.** 677 + 380	**4.** 406 + 312
5. 951 + 123	**6.** 705 + 357	**7.** 824 + 199	**8.** 901 + 699
9. 333 + 178	**10.** 101 + 752	**11.** 509 + 456	**12.** 712 + 55
13. 278 + 333	**14.** 158 + 207	**15.** 199 + 682	**16.** 999 + 715
17. 508 + 349	**18.** 724 + 924	**19.** 911 + 667	**20.** 507 + 133

Lesson 6

3-Digit 3-Row Addition - Regrouping

To add multiple digit numbers together, start in the ones place and then use basic addition rules. When the number equals ten or more the first digit carries over to the next spot. This is called **regrouping**.

Solve the problems below using regrouping.

1. 209	**2.** 456	**3.** 652	**4.** 572	**5.** 711
158	41	189	267	209
+ 472	+ 137	+ 305	+ 453	+ 374
839				
6. 455	**7.** 501	**8.** 782	**9.** 955	**10.** 389
126	472	106	572	411
+ 907	+ 904	+ 313	+ 117	+ 354
11. 111	**12.** 254	**13.** 715	**14.** 742	**15.** 958
684	906	355	279	144
+ 243	+ 145	+ 742	+ 109	+ 302
16. 621	**17.** 322	**18.** 752	**19.** 884	**20.** 308
435	532	962	222	144
+ 905	+ 814	+ 103	+ 606	+ 722

3-Digit 3-Row Addition - Regrouping 2

To add multiple digit numbers together, start in the ones place and then use basic addition rules. When the number equals ten or more the first digit carries over to the next spot. This is called **regrouping**.

Solve the problems below using regrouping.

1. 643	**2.** 119	**3.** 307	**4.** 678	**5.** 819
207	875	458	152	644
+ 318	+ 40	+ 156	+ 306	+ 278
6. 339	**7.** 712	**8.** 181	**9.** 899	**10.** 165
107	263	396	295	980
+ 389	+ 140	+ 15	+ 590	+ 263
11. 752	**12.** 157	**13.** 208	**14.** 257	**15.** 700
310	682	489	367	973
+ 726	+ 898	+ 912	+ 6	+ 275
16. 661	**17.** 313	**18.** 985	**19.** 785	**20.** 222
894	578	405	246	746
+ 64	+ 149	+ 123	+ 385	+ 118

Lesson 7

4-Digit Addition - Regrouping

Solve the problems below using regrouping.

1. 6895 + 5406 12301	**2.** 1259 + 9502	**3.** 9543 + 7845	**4.** 4051 + 1150
5. 8507 + 9847	**6.** 3250 + 406	**7.** 2470 + 3357	**8.** 1589 + 6875
9. 5579 + 6077	**10.** 1089 + 2786	**11.** 7750 + 597	**12.** 3378 + 4508
13. 6917 + 7502	**14.** 4329 + 999	**15.** 9948 + 113	**16.** 4705 + 4866
17. 1580 + 3987	**18.** 2778 + 4891	**19.** 5576 + 569	**20.** 3520 + 1339

Lesson 8

4-Digit 3-Row Addition - Regrouping

Solve the problems below using regrouping.

1. 1091 2157 + 3267 6515	**2.** 9815 4803 + 2216	**3.** 3891 1259 + 7520	**4.** 2552 8406 + 2271
5. 5330 1211 + 9801	**6.** 4881 2009 + 1987	**7.** 3072 1650 + 1578	**8.** 1985 8105 + 1776
9. 9841 2750 + 1349	**10.** 5400 7501 + 3814	**11.** 7072 6152 + 1785	**12.** 1707 1804 + 2950
13. 2400 3962 + 8815	**14.** 6074 1255 + 8079	**15.** 8180 2755 + 2577	**16.** 9064 9607 + 6074
17. 4911 2757 + 3025	**18.** 5787 6962 + 1570	**19.** 7705 5321 + 1766	**20.** 3033 1447 + 9632

Lesson 9

5-Digit Addition - Regrouping

Solve the problems below using regrouping.

1. 15,801 + 35,847 = 51648

2. 75,211 + 25,786

3. 89,057 + 11,059

4. 33,520 + 6,579

5. 40,517 + 12,523

6. 74,259 + 69,805

7. 94,521 + 7,089

8. 30,671 + 31,337

9. 45,994 + 27,881

10. 65,817 + 5,847

11. 11,072 + 36,698

12. 32,501 + 4,879

13. 90,117 + 15,257

14. 85,024 + 96,312

15. 57,781 + 5,690

16. 78,521 + 36,901

17. 58,520 + 57,936

18. 30,258 + 28,527

19. 78,269 + 10,254

20. 63,391 + 60,582

Lesson 10

5-Digit 2-Column Addition - Regrouping

Solve the problems below using regrouping.

1. 68,502 + 35,847	**2.** 32,000 + 17,815	**3.** 49,215 + 21,589	**4.** 65,107 + 42,238
5. 86,011 + 32,997	**6.** 91,058 + 15,211	**7.** 70,122 + 62,939	**8.** 29,006 + 11,271
9. 55,127 + 17,568	**10.** 25,087 + 9,175	**11.** 49,186 + 23,250	**12.** 95,118 + 3,935
13. 77,117 + 59,990	**14.** 45,710 + 36,303	**15.** 67,181 + 2,628	**16.** 82,207 + 60,845
17. 45,387 + 36,105	**18.** 77,007 + 11,367	**19.** 60,117 + 46,289	**20.** 84,999 + 26,111

Chapter 3 - Subtraction

Lesson 1

2-Digit Subtraction - Borrowing 1

To subtract and borrow , start with the ones's column. If the bottom number is of a greater value, you have to borrow from the next column.

	Ten's	One's
Step 1: If the bottom number is a greater value than the top number, you need to borrow.	8 - 1	4 9
Step 2: Borrow 10 from the next column. Reducing the 8 to 7 and increasing 4 to 14. Now we are ready to subtract.	7 ~~8~~ - 1	[1]4 9 5
Step 3: Finish by subtracting the numbers in the ten's column.	7 ~~8~~ - 1 6	[1]4 9 5

Use borrowing to solve the problems below.

1. 35 - 6 29	**2.** 54 - 28	**3.** 83 - 4	**4.** 42 - 15	**5.** 56 - 9
6. 41 - 5	**7.** 82 - 59	**8.** 16 - 7	**9.** 71 - 3	**10.** 52 - 28
11. 87 - 59	**12.** 34 - 6	**13.** 72 - 35	**14.** 21 - 2	**15.** 91 - 44

2-Digit Subtraction - Borrowing 2

Use borrowing to solve the problems below.

1. 44	**2.** 64	**3.** 37	**4.** 66	**5.** 55
− 35	− 5	− 19	− 7	− 17
6. 50	**7.** 88	**8.** 25	**9.** 72	**10.** 32
− 27	− 36	− 16	− 53	− 29
11. 44	**12.** 90	**13.** 29	**14.** 65	**15.** 78
− 17	− 76	− 14	− 44	− 53
16. 63	**17.** 50	**18.** 37	**19.** 99	**20.** 52
− 49	− 9	− 18	− 64	− 23

2-Digit Subtraction - Borrowing - Fill in the Blanks

Use borrowing to solve the problems below.

Problem	Top	Subtract	Answer
1.	48	- 29	1□
2.	25	- 7	1□
3.	60	- □	51
4.	36	- 8	□8
5.	77	- □9	58
6.	60	- □3	27
7.	94	- 46	□8
8.	15	- 6	□
9.	□2	- 9	13
10.	30	- 1□	13
11.	72	- □4	48
12.	20	- □2	8
13.	51	- 16	□5
14.	46	- 9	□7
15.	32	- □9	13
16.	67	- 39	□8
17.	12	- □	6
18.	24	- □9	5
19.	71	- □5	16
20.	47	- 19	□8

Lesson 2

Subtraction Word Problems

Use subtraction to solve the problems below.

1. Selena is a good soccer player. This season she has taken 38 shots at the goal and made 6 of them. How many shots has she missed this season?

2. Billy just can't stop eating cookies. He had 62 cookies in his jar. He ate 18 of them. How many cookies are left in the jar?

3. Aida loves baseball. She has gone to 103 games in her life. 39 were away games. How many were home games?

4. Jonathan has collected 47 snowflakes today, but 23 of them have already melted. How many snowflakes does Jonathan have left?

Lesson 3

3-Digit Subtraction - Borrowing 1

To subtract and borrow, start with the ones's column. If the bottom number is of a greater value, you have to borrow from the next column.

Step 1: Any time the bottom number in a column is of greater value than the top number, you need to borrow.

100's	10's	1's
7	6	3
- 4	8	5

Step 2: Borrow 10 from the next column. This reduces the 6 to 5 and increases the numbers in the first column from 3 to 13.

100's	10's	1's
7	~~6~~ 5	13
- 4	8	5

Step 3: Now we need to borrow 10 from the hundred's column. This reduces the 7 to 6 and increases the numbers in the ten's column from 5 to 15.

100's	10's	1's
~~7~~ 6	~~6~~ 15	13
- 4	8	5

Step 4: Finish by subtracting the numbers in all the columns.

100's	10's	1's
~~7~~ 6	~~6~~ 15	13
- 4	8	5
2	7	8

Use borrowing to solve the problems below.

1. 289 - 134 = 155

2. 412 - 389

3. 518 - 79

4. 962 - 473

5. 412 - 273

6. 652 - 386

7. 179 - 83

8. 712 - 554

9. 369 - 254

10. 811 - 632

11. 895 - 67

12. 337 - 287

13. 615 - 457

14. 906 - 687

15. 675 - 399

3-Digit Subtraction - Borrowing 2

Use borrowing to solve the problems below.

1. 296 - 147	**2.** 472 - 228	**3.** 915 - 455	**4.** 371 - 52
5. 612 - 377	**6.** 501 - 458	**7.** 715 - 207	**8.** 185 - 152
9. 999 - 342	**10.** 307 - 158	**11.** 844 - 599	**12.** 199 - 57
13. 689 - 394	**14.** 472 - 59	**15.** 315 - 199	**16.** 578 - 419
17. 972 - 859	**18.** 572 - 289	**19.** 911 - 487	**20.** 308 - 157

3-Digit Subtraction - Borrowing - Fill in the Blanks

Use borrowing to fill in the blanks below.

1. 428 - 305 1□3	**2.** 577 - □07 370	**3.** 671 - 1□5 486	**4.** 780 - 339 □41
5. 719 - 45□ 267	**6.** 672 - □35 537	**7.** 517 - 365 1□2	**8.** 217 - 82 13□
9. 857 - 369 4□8	**10.** 624 - 29 □95	**11.** 78□ - 345 440	**12.** 266 - 117 1□9
13. 456 - 3□5 141	**14.** 206 - 12□ 85	**15.** 367 - 27□ 92	**16.** 785 - 316 46□
17. 454 - □99 255	**18.** 720 - 367 □53	**19.** 894 - 176 7□8	**20.** 269 - □56 113

Lesson 4

4-Digit Subtraction - Borrowing 1

Use what you learned about borrowing to solve the problems below.

1. 6,432 − 5,320 = 1,112	**2.** 2,675 − 1,564	**3.** 4,233 − 452	**4.** 5,428 − 2,649
5. 1,995 − 239	**6.** 7,321 − 834	**7.** 9,211 − 1,700	**8.** 3,946 − 1,682
9. 2,463 − 1,939	**10.** 8,959 − 3,274	**11.** 1,295 − 968	**12.** 9,942 − 7,895
13. 7,542 − 2,907	**14.** 3,649 − 1,590	**15.** 9,864 − 4,389	**16.** 3,888 − 999
17. 5,001 − 3,547	**18.** 1,775 − 859	**19.** 3,880 − 1,125	**20.** 9,567 − 6,820

4-Digit Subtraction - Borrowing 2

Use what you learned about borrowing to solve the problems below.

1. 3,291 − 1,675	**2.** 7,052 − 5,894	**3.** 1,020 − 532	**4.** 9,214 − 7,580
5. 2,856 − 1,697	**6.** 5,441 − 2,583	**7.** 7,654 − 5,439	**8.** 9,201 − 2,550
9. 6,549 − 3,058	**10.** 1,205 − 317	**11.** 4,053 − 1,589	**12.** 9,087 − 4,682
13. 3,001 − 1,892	**14.** 9,897 − 5,432	**15.** 6,901 − 3,784	**16.** 5,338 − 2,058
17. 8,071 − 3,687	**18.** 9,001 − 5,592	**19.** 4,207 − 2,072	**20.** 9,991 − 3,058

Lesson 5

5-Digit Subtraction - Borrowing 1

Use what you learned about borrowing to solve the problems below.

1. 62,734	**2.** 45,689	**3.** 90,254	**4.** 12,097
- 49,586	- 29,875	- 67,702	- 7,850
13,148			

5. 80,775	**6.** 37,820	**7.** 54,519	**8.** 70,421
- 24,078	- 9,507	- 20,179	- 34,219

9. 21,997	**10.** 95,327	**11.** 40,871	**12.** 10,037
- 1,509	- 70,587	- 27,815	- 5,871

13. 78,510	**14.** 37,540	**15.** 50,574	**16.** 29,992
- 40,327	- 1,058	- 27,899	- 10,871

17. 40,087	**18.** 78,560	**19.** 12,687	**20.** 45,230
- 21,589	- 52,278	- 11,339	- 7,854

5-Digit Subtraction - Borrowing 2

Use what you learned about borrowing to solve the problems below.

1. 13,489 - 11,792	**2.** 86,371 - 45,927	**3.** 50,762 - 36,875	**4.** 38,792 - 15,806
5. 21,743 - 6,158	**6.** 35,309 - 9,507	**7.** 98,051 - 65,473	**8.** 66,259 - 29,402
9. 32,278 - 14,369	**10.** 20,897 - 5,098	**11.** 55,807 - 34,568	**12.** 97,051 - 65,204
13. 65,790 - 22,903	**14.** 10,854 - 9,661	**15.** 77,059 - 40,572	**16.** 85,220 - 33,078
17. 36,754 - 18,265	**18.** 54,587 - 33,058	**19.** 63,017 - 45,582	**20.** 70,000 - 25,783

Chapter 4 - Decimals

Lesson 1

Adding Decimals 1

Adding decimals is like most normal addition. You just have to remember to line up the decimals.

Hint: Decimal points always go at the end of a whole number (3 = 3.0 or 3.00)

Example: Add 2.43, 4.5 and 3

Step 1: Line up the numbers	**Step 2:** Add zeros	**Step 3:** Find the total
$\begin{array}{r} 2.43 \\ 4.5 \\ +\ 3 \\ \hline \end{array}$	$\begin{array}{r} 2.43 \\ 4.50 \\ +\ 3.00 \\ \hline \end{array}$	$\begin{array}{r} 2.43 \\ 4.50 \\ +\ 3.00 \\ \hline 9.93 \end{array}$

Line up the numbers and solve the problems below.
Show your work in the boxes.

1: 1.21 + 2.33 + .05

$$\begin{array}{r} 1.21 \\ 2.33 \\ +\ .05 \\ \hline 3.59 \end{array}$$

2: 4 + 1.63 + 2.20

3: .24 + 4.87 + 11

4: 7.12 + 2.04 + 5

5: 9.11 + .43 + .89

6: 64 + 8.79 + 1.57

Adding Decimals 2

Use what you learned about adding numbers with decimals to find the totals to the questions below. Show your work in the boxes.

1: 9.34 + .44 + 6.17

2: 590 + 2.49 + 71.99

3: .04 + 3.03 + 24.42

4: 3.18 + 2.01 + 35.78

5: 584.11 + 789.8 + .50

6: 584 + 1.29 + 36.99

7: 6.08 + 3.46 + .99

8: 15 + 37.16 + 2.09

9: 7.89 + 1.11 + 109

Lesson 2

Adding Money 1

The rules that we learned for adding decimals is how we add money.

$$\begin{array}{r} 2.69 \\ +\ 5.11 \\ \hline 7.80 \end{array} \quad = \quad \begin{array}{r} \$2.69 \\ +\ \$5.11 \\ \hline \$7.80 \end{array}$$

Find the totals below.

1. $\begin{array}{r} \$1.40 \\ +\ \$3.63 \\ \hline \$5.03 \end{array}$ **2.** $\begin{array}{r} \$7.18 \\ +\ \$4.45 \\ \hline \end{array}$ **3.** $\begin{array}{r} \$2.50 \\ +\ \$6.72 \\ \hline \end{array}$ **4.** $\begin{array}{r} \$1.15 \\ +\ \$5.25 \\ \hline \end{array}$

5. $\begin{array}{r} \$9.40 \\ +\ \$3.35 \\ \hline \end{array}$ **6.** $\begin{array}{r} \$10.45 \\ +\$11.82 \\ \hline \end{array}$ **7.** $\begin{array}{r} \$20.15 \\ +\ \$2.38 \\ \hline \end{array}$ **8.** $\begin{array}{r} \$14.05 \\ +\ \$5.59 \\ \hline \end{array}$

9. $\begin{array}{r} \$6.55 \\ \$1.47 \\ +\ \$3.91 \\ \hline \end{array}$ **10.** $\begin{array}{r} \$2.13 \\ \$4.75 \\ +\ \$5.59 \\ \hline \end{array}$ **11.** $\begin{array}{r} \$1.55 \\ \$8.09 \\ +\ \$6.32 \\ \hline \end{array}$ **12.** $\begin{array}{r} \$2.77 \\ \$8.59 \\ +\ \$3.40 \\ \hline \end{array}$

13. $\begin{array}{r} \$17.09 \\ \$1.99 \\ +\ \$3.20 \\ \hline \end{array}$ **14.** $\begin{array}{r} \$10.33 \\ \$8.95 \\ +\ \$1.27 \\ \hline \end{array}$ **15.** $\begin{array}{r} \$18.17 \\ \$9.49 \\ +\ \$7.55 \\ \hline \end{array}$ **16.** $\begin{array}{r} \$12.35 \\ \$2.78 \\ +\ \$5.15 \\ \hline \end{array}$

Adding Money 2

Find the totals below.

1. $9.32
+ $4.13
$13.45

2. $6.91
+ $3.57

3. $8.10
+ $2.36

4. $5.55
+ $1.35

5. $77.02
+$62.23

6. $50.85
+$32.04

7. $29.77
+$12.75

8. $82.26
+$40.11

9. $16.88
$91.05
+$53.12

10. $55.30
$30.99
+ $7.15

11. $62.10
$1.99
+ $28.50

12. $39.03
$20.27
+$51.11

13. $100.33
$55.70
+ $7.16

14. $555.46
$71.26
+ $3.90

15. $123.50
$40.49
+ $8.17

16. $609.99
$24.35
+ $5.22

17. $759.09
$208.99
+$177.20

18. $405.00
$620.50
+$378.99

19. $907.89
$182.63
+$330.17

20. $365.11
$657.78
+$307.40

Adding Money 3

Find the totals below.

1. \$6.05 + \$4.11	**2.** \$3.94 + \$2.29	**3.** \$9.99 + \$7.65	**4.** \$5.25 + \$8.39
5. \$8.38 + \$9.12	**6.** \$66.45 + \$29.82	**7.** \$95.30 + \$12.65	**8.** \$84.94 + \$17.05
9. \$29.75, \$1.40 + \$8.97	**10.** \$20.51, \$45.68 + \$9.42	**11.** \$95.12, \$58.63 + \$17.08	**12.** \$62.22, \$30.52 + \$68.67
13. \$152.78, \$126.36 + \$75.11	**14.** \$429.33, \$639.95 + \$115.27	**15.** \$290.24, \$907.57 + \$333.03	**16.** \$369.67, \$105.18 + \$59.07
17. \$625.99, \$470.75 + \$364.23	**18.** \$129.00, \$650.70 + \$321.33	**19.** \$459.99, \$630.01 + \$780.40	**20.** \$111.27, \$252.96 + \$639.57

Lesson 3

Adding Decimals Word Problems

Solve the problems below.

1. Jimmie's water gun can hold 30.08 ounces of water. Steven's water gun can hold 22.56 ounces. How many ounces of water do they have together?

____

2. Sara walks every afternoon. On Monday she walked 2.3 miles. On Tuesday she walked 1.8 miles. On Wednesday she walked 3.1 miles. How many miles did she walk in total?

____

3. Mickey loves to race his bike. In race one he had a finishing time of 13.38 minutes. In race two he had a finishing time of 12.58 minutes. In race three he had a finishing time of 12.32 minutes. What was his total time for all the races?

____

4. Mary can carry 6.75 pounds of dirt in her wagon. Mark can carry 8.25 pounds in his wagon. How much dirt can they carry in total?

____

Lesson 4

Rounding Decimals 1

To round numbers with decimal points look at the numbers to right of the decimal. If it has a value of higher than 5 round the number to the left of the decimal up.

6.8 = 7

If the number to the right of the decimal is less than 5, round the number down.

6.3 = 6

Round each decimal to the nearest whole number.

1. 92.8 = 93 **2.** 12.5 = ____

3. 33.1 = ____ **4.** 24.9 = ____

5. 57.7 = ____ **6.** 65.1 = ____

7. 82.5 = ____ **8.** 41.6 = ____

9. 68.6 = ____ **10.** 20.4 = ____

11. 34.2 = ____ **12.** 31.8 = ____

13. 76.7 = ____ **13.** 72.2 = ____

15. 12.3 = ____ **16.** 43.7 = ____

17. 45.8 = ____ **18.** 55.9 = ____

19. 21.4 = ____ **20.** 19.3 = ____

Rounding Decimals 2

Round each decimal to the nearest whole number.

1. 892.86 = ____ **2.** 112.51 = ____

3. 133.41 = ____ **4.** 24.9 = ____

5. 57.38 = ____ **6.** 765.12 = ____

7. 22.23 = ____ **8.** 341.64 = ____

9. 318.34 = ____ **10.** 920.48 = ____

11. 94.19 = ____ **12.** 31.83 = ____

13. 56.77 = ____ **14.** 672.26= ____

15. 812.62 = ____ **16.** 543.71 = ____

17. 35.21 = ____ **18.** 811.95 = ____

19. 121.84 = ____ **20.** 698.34 = ____

Lesson 5

Subtracting Decimals 1

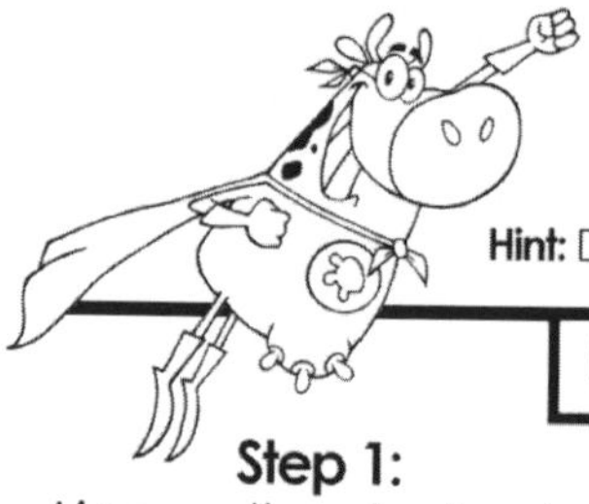

Subtracting decimals is like normal subtraction.
You just have to remember to line up the decimals.

Hint: Decimal points always go at the end of a whole number (6 = 6.0 or 6.00)

Example: Subtract 5.7 from 9.39

Step 1: Line up the decimals.	**Step 2:** Add zeros and borrow when needed.	**Step 3:** Subtract all the numbers.
9.39 − 5.7	8 ~~9~~.[1]39 − 5.70	8 ~~9~~.[1]39 − 5.70 3.69

Line up the numbers and solve the problems below.
Show your work in the boxes.

1. 6.05 - 3.89

6.05
− 3.89
2.16

2. 48.27 - 13.65

3. 8.55 - 3.9

4. 331 - 4.72

5. 902.22 - 47.79

6. 75.5 - 6.51

Subtracting Decimals 2

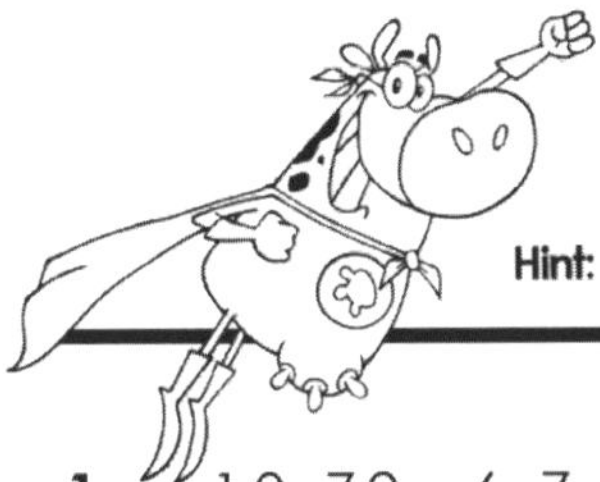

Subtracting decimals is like normal subtraction.
You just have to remember to line up the decimals.

Hint: Decimal points always go at the end of a whole number (6 = 6.0 or 6.00)

1. 10.72 - 6.7

2. 72.7 - 22.35

3. 105.11 - 90.3

4. 56 - 13 .09

5. 44.22 - 42.49

6. 589.5 - 7.89

7. 17.49 - 9.06

8. 632.59 - 377.44

9. 808.05 - 6.9

Lesson 6
Subtracting Money 1

Now that you know how to subtract decimals, use what you learned to answer these money problems.

6.89		$6.89
- 4.32	=	- $4.32
2.57		$2.57

Subtract the amounts below.

1. $4.58 - $2.11 $2.47	**2.** $8.49 - $5.35	**3.** $6.50 - $3.32	**4.** $9.75 - $7.89
5. $9.90 - $8.75	**6.** $2.93 - $1.08	**7.** $6.15 - $2.38	**8.** $7.38 - $5.08
9. $4.15 - $1.02	**10.** $5.65 - $2.36	**11.** $3.46 - $3.07	**12.** $9.15 - $6.10
13. $13.04 - $8.25	**14.** $31.35 - $9.07	**15.** $15.89 - $2.35	**16.** $17.38 - $6.40
17. $16.82 - $9.05	**18.** $21.93 - $7.08	**19.** $10.15 - $2.38	**20.** $20.00 -$10.99

Subtracting Money 2

Subtract the amounts below.

1. \$10.13 - \$2.29	**2.** \$25.55 - \$5.02	**3.** \$17.89 - \$3.39	**4.** \$20.15 - \$7.09
5. \$45.77 -\$15.36	**6.** \$23.01 -\$17.99	**7.** \$39.50 -\$27.28	**8.** \$26.55 -\$11.17
9. \$58.37 -\$49.99	**10.** \$79.44 -\$60.76	**11.** \$62.08 -\$34.13	**12.** \$95.35 -\$17.37
13. \$100.04 -\$68.68	**14.** \$216.42 -\$84.36	**15.** \$199.55 -\$35.23	**16.** \$956.11 -\$25.71
17. \$209.44 -\$155.88	**18.** \$356.77 -\$208.05	**19.** \$589.33 - \$199.07	**20.** \$250.99 -\$217.95

Lesson 7

Subtracting Decimals Word Problems

Use subtraction to solve the problems below.

1. Pete wants a new teddy bear. His mom is going to help him buy one. A new bear costs $19.50. Pete has $7.32. How much money does he need to get from mom?

____

2. Tammy wants a new jump rope. She has $3.78. The jump rope costs $6.99. How much more money does she need?

____

3. Randy and John want a new toy truck. The toy truck costs $13.75. Randy has $4.15 and John has $6.42. How much more money do they need?

____

4. Eric sold his old pogo stick for $5.89. A new one costs $35.99. How much more money does Eric need?

____

Chapter 5 - Multiplication

Lesson 1

Multiplication

Multiplication Table

x	1	2	3	4	5	6	7	8	9	10
1	1	2	3	4	5	6	7	8	9	10
2	2	4	6	8	10	12	14	16	18	20
3	3	6	9	12	15	18	21	24	27	30
4	4	8	12	16	20	24	28	32	36	40
5	5	10	15	20	25	30	35	40	45	50
6	6	12	18	24	30	36	42	48	54	60
7	7	14	21	28	35	42	49	56	63	70
8	8	16	24	32	40	48	56	64	72	80
9	9	18	27	36	45	54	63	72	81	90
10	10	20	30	40	50	60	70	80	90	100

Lesson 2

Multiplication Tables 1

X	1	2	3
1	1	2	3
2	2	4	6

This is a multiplication table. Multiply the numbers in the top row by the numbers in the side row.

1.

X	1	2	3	4	5
6					
7					
8					

2.

X	7	8	9
4			
5			
6			
7			
8			

3.

X	9	10	11
7			
8			
9			
10			
11			

4.

X	2	3	4	5	6
20					
25					
27					

Lesson 3

Multiplying 1-Digit Numbers by 2-Digit Numbers

To multiply a one-digit number by a two-digit number, start in the ones place and then use basic multiplication rules.

Step 1:
Multiply the numbers in the one's place

	Ten's	One's
	4	3
x		2
		6

Step 2:
Multiply the numbers in the ten's place

	Ten's	One's
	4	3
x		2
	8	6

Solve the problems below.

1. 24 x 2 = 48

2. 31 x 3

3. 43 x 2

4. 11 x 7

5. 11 x 5

6. 44 x 2

7. 11 x 9

8. 18 x 1

9. 21 x 4

10. 22 x 3

Lesson 4

Multiplying by 10s

Multiplying by ten is just like regular two-digit number multiplication, but there is just one extra step. You bring the zero down first, this adds it to the end of the number.

	Hundred's	Ten's	One's
		5	4
x		1	0
			0

	Hundred's	Ten's	One's
		5	4
x		1	0
		4	0

	Hundred's	Ten's	One's
		5	4
x		1	0
	5	4	0

Solve the problems below.

1. 26 x 10 = 260

2. 71 x 10

3. 67 x 10

4. 22 x 10

5. 38 x 10

6. 84 x 10

7. 19 x 10

8. 18 x 10

9. 94 x 10

10. 29 x 10

Multiplying by 10s 2

Multiplying by ten is just like regular two-digit multiplication, but there is just one extra step. You bring the zero down first; this adds it to the end of the number.

Solve the problems below by multiplying the numbers by ten.

1. 44 x 10

2. 89 x 20

3. 52 x 50

4. 13 x 90

5. 48 x 30

6. 49 x 20

7. 18 x 10

8. 33 x 80

9. 92 x 50

10. 57 x 70

11. 67 x 10

12. 21 x 60

13. 27 x 10

14. 75 x 90

15. 50 x 30

16. 66 x 20

17. 82 x 10

18. 55 x 30

19. 45 x 50

20. 61 x 90

Multiplying by 10 3

Multiplying by ten is just like regular two-digit multiplication, but there is just one extra step. You bring the zero down first; this adds it to the end of the number.

Solve the problems below by filling in the blanks.

1. 82 x 10 = 820

2. 59 x 10 = ____

3. 36 x 10 = ____

4. 91 x 10 = ____

5. 27 x 10 = ____

6. 60 x 10 = ____

7. 10 x 95 = ____

8. 10 x 89 = ____

9. 10 x 43 = ____

10. 10 x 27 = ____

11. 10 x 56 = ____

12. 10 x 39 = ____

13. ____ x 10 = 750

14. 12 x ____ = 120

15. 10 x ____ = 880

16. ____ x 10 = 620

17. ____ x 10 = 590

18. 10 x ____ = 10

Lesson 5

Multiplying 1-Digit Numbers by 2-Digit Numbers - Regrouping

To multiply a one-digit number by a two-digit number with regrouping, start in the ones place and then use basic multiplication rules. When the number equals ten or more, the first digit carries over to the next spot. This is called **regrouping**.

Step 1: Multiply the numbers in the ones column and carry the first digit over to the tens column.

Hundreds	Tens	Ones
	2	
	4	7
X		3
		[1]

3x7=21

Step 2: Multiply the digit in at the bottom of the ones column by the digit in the tens column and add the regrouped number.

Hundreds	Tens	Ones
	2	
	+ 4	7
X		3
	[4]	1

4x3=12 Then 12+2=14

Step 3: The one then carries over to the hundreds place.

Hundreds	Tens	Ones
	2	
	4	7
X		3
[1]	4	1

Answer = 141

Solve the problems below.

1. 46 x 2 = 92

2. 58 x 7

3. 43 x 4

4. 87 x 3

5. 36 x 5

6. 44 x 5

7. 32 x 9

8. 55 x 9

9. 99 x 2

10. 59 x 6

Multiplying 1-Digit numbers by 2-Digit numbers - Regrouping 2

To multiply a one-digit number by a two-digit number with regrouping, start in the ones place and then use basic multiplication rules. When the number equals ten or more the first digit carries over to the next spot. This is called **regrouping**.

Solve the problems below.

1. 28 x 3	**2.** 75 x 2	**3.** 13 x 4	**4.** 62 x 9	**5.** 99 x 2
6. 85 x 5	**7.** 26 x 7	**8.** 44 x 4	**9.** 96 x 3	**10.** 57 x 6
11. 72 x 2	**12.** 33 x 8	**13.** 82 x 5	**14.** 29 x 9	**15.** 66 x 4
16. 59 x 4	**17.** 26 x 9	**18.** 54 x 7	**19.** 95 x 5	**20.** 46 x 6

Lesson 6

Multiplying 1-Digit Numbers by 3-Digit Numbers - Regrouping

To multiply a one-digit number by a three-digit number, start in the ones place and then use basic multiplication rules.

Step 1:	Step 2:	Step 3:
First multiply the top digit in the one's column by the bottom digit in the one's column.	Next multiply the digit in the ten's column by the bottom digit in the one's column.	Next multiply the digit in the hundred's column by the bottom digit in the one's column.
100's / 10's / 1's 2 3 3 x 3 9	100's / 10's / 1's 2 3 3 x 3 9 9	100's / 10's / 1's 2 3 3 x 3 6 9 9
3x3=9	3x3=9	2x3=6 **Answer** = 699

Solve the problems below.

1. 142 x 2 = 284

2. 221 x 3

3. 341 x 2

4. 121 x 4

5. 698 x 1

6. 212 x 4

7. 132 x 3

8. 233 x 2

9. 232 x 3

10. 141 x 2

11. 212 x 3

12. 112 x 3

Multiplying 1-Digit numbers by 3-Digit numbers - Regrouping 2

To multiply a one-digit number by a three-digit number, start in the ones place and then use basic multiplication rules. Dont forget to use the regrouping rules you learned in the previous sections.

Solve the problems below.

1. 651 x 2	**2.** 221 x 3	**3.** 341 x 5	**4.** 433 x 4
5. 698 x 9	**6.** 212 x 4	**7.** 132 x 3	**8.** 233 x 8
9. 232 x 9	**10.** 549 x 2	**11.** 689 x 7	**12.** 599 x 5
13. 986 x 8	**14.** 123 x 6	**15.** 977 x 4	**16.** 222 x 5
17. 685 x 4	**18.** 304 x 8	**19.** 960 x 9	**20.** 795 x 2

Lesson 7

Multiplying 2-Digit numbers by 3-Digit numbers - Regrouping

To multiply a two-digit number by a two-digit number, start in the ones place and then use basic multiplication and addition rules. Dont forget to use what you learned about regrouping.

1. Multiply by the **ones** multiplier.

100's	10's	1's
	2 +	
	4	6
x	2	4
1	0	4

4 is the first multiplier

4 x 46 = 104

2. Multiply by the **tens** multiplier.

100's	10's	1's
	1 +	
	4	6
x	2	4
1	8	4
+ 9	2	0

20 is the second multiplier

20 x 46 = 104

3. Add the products.

100's	10's	1's
	4	6
x	2	4
1	8	4
+ 9	2	0
1 1	0	4

Add the two products

184 + 920 = 1104

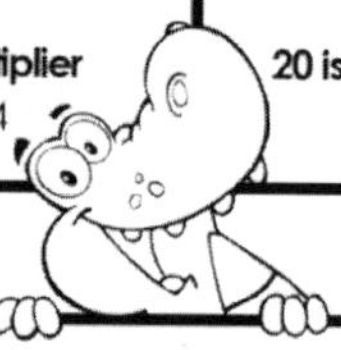

Solve the problems below.

1. 49 x 15 = 245 + 490 = 735

2. 13 x 12

3. 54 x 22

4. 72 x 45

5. 38 x 25

6. 84 x 55

7. 69 x 37

8. 29 x 23

9. 79 x 56

10. 99 x 56

Multiplying 2-Digit numbers by 3-Digit numbers - Regrouping 2

Solve the problems below.

1. 67 x 49	**2.** 24 x 15	**3.** 49 x 36	**4.** 29 x 27	**5.** 44 x 39
6. 84 x 60	**7.** 66 x 34	**8.** 87 x 11	**9.** 99 x 49	**10.** 70 x 59
11. 39 x 27	**12.** 24 x 17	**13.** 86 x 37	**14.** 11 x 83	**15.** 97 x 57
16. 55 x 90	**17.** 75 x 22	**18.** 68 x 43	**19.** 92 x 37	**20.** 19 x 26

Chapter 6 - Division

Lesson 1

Division

- Division is a way to find out how many times one number is counted in another number.
- The $\div$ sign means " divided by".
- Another way to divide is to use $\overline{)}$.
- The dividend is the larger number that is divided by the smaller number, the divisor.
- The answer of a division problem is called the quotient.

$\div$ means divide

$$6 \div 2 = 3$$

dividend (6) **divisor** (2) **quotient** (3)

- $6 \div 2 = 3$ is read "6 divided by 2 is equal to 3".
- In $6 \div 2 = 3$, the divisor is 2, the dividend is 6 and the quotient is 3.

$\overline{)}$ means divide

$$\begin{array}{r} 5 \\ 2\overline{)10} \end{array}$$

divisor (2) **dividend** (10) **quotient** (5)

- $\begin{array}{r} 5 \\ 2\overline{)10} \end{array}$ is read "10 divided by 2 is equal to 5".
- In $\begin{array}{r} 5 \\ 2\overline{)10} \end{array}$, the divisor is 2, the dividend is 10 and the quotient is 5.

Lesson 2

Basic Division

Divide these problems.

1. $\begin{array}{r}3\\7\overline{)21}\end{array}$ **2.** $6\overline{)48}$ **3.** $2\overline{)12}$ **4.** $7\overline{)28}$

5. $4\overline{)36}$ **6.** $3\overline{)21}$ **7.** $7\overline{)21}$ **8.** $5\overline{)40}$

9. $5\overline{)15}$ **10.** $2\overline{)6}$ **11.** $8\overline{)72}$ **12.** $10\overline{)100}$

13. $8\overline{)32}$ **14.** $5\overline{)25}$ **15.** $5\overline{)5}$ **16.** $8\overline{)88}$

17. $8\overline{)56}$ **18.** $5\overline{)75}$ **19.** $3\overline{)9}$ **20.** $4\overline{)32}$

Lesson 3

Division with Remainders 1

- Sometimes groups of objects or numbers cannot be divided into equal groups.
- The number left over in a division problem is called the remainder.
- The remainder must be smaller than the divisor.

If we divide 13 into groups of 5, you get 2 equal groups and 3 left over. These are the **remainders**.

This is how you write it out. →

$$\begin{array}{r} 2\,r\,3 \\ 5\overline{)13} \\ -10 \\ \hline 3 \end{array}$$

Divide these problems, some may not have remainders.

1. $\begin{array}{r} 2\,r\,2 \\ 3\overline{)8} \\ -6 \\ \hline 2 \end{array}$ **2.** $7\overline{)35}$ **3.** $6\overline{)25}$ **4.** $8\overline{)39}$

5. $5\overline{)52}$ **6.** $9\overline{)85}$ **7.** $5\overline{)61}$ **8.** $3\overline{)43}$

Division with Remainders 2

Divide these problems, some may not have remainders.

1. $2\overline{)9}$ **2.** $6\overline{)15}$ **3.** $2\overline{)33}$

4. $3\overline{)15}$ **5.** $5\overline{)27}$ **6.** $9\overline{)44}$

7. $9\overline{)58}$ **8.** $7\overline{)32}$ **9.** $6\overline{)40}$

10. $2\overline{)77}$ **11.** $8\overline{)99}$ **12.** $2\overline{)61}$

13. $8\overline{)66}$ **14.** $5\overline{)62}$ **15.** $8\overline{)49}$

Lesson 4

Division - Fill in the Blanks

Use division to fill in the boxes on the problems below.

1. $4\overline{)\,36\,}$ = 9
2. $6\overline{)\,\square\,}$ = 9
3. $4\overline{)\,\square\,}$ = 15
4. $5\overline{)\,\square\,}$ = 20
5. $3\overline{)\,\square\,}$ = 2
6. $7\overline{)\,\square\,}$ = 7
7. $2\overline{)\,\square\,}$ = 5
8. $9\overline{)\,\square\,}$ = 5
9. $8\overline{)\,\square\,}$ = 8
10. $9\overline{)\,\square\,}$ = 32
11. $7\overline{)\,\square\,}$ = 9
12. $3\overline{)\,\square\,}$ = 11
13. $6\overline{)\,\square\,}$ = 9
14. $4\overline{)\,\square\,}$ = 6

Division - Fill in the Blanks 2

Use division to fill in the boxes on the problems below.

1. $\boxed{8}\overline{)48}$, quotient: 6
2. $\boxed{}\overline{)77}$, quotient: 7
3. $\boxed{}\overline{)35}$, quotient: 15
4. $\boxed{}\overline{)12}$, quotient: 2
5. $\boxed{}\overline{)45}$, quotient: 9
6. $\boxed{}\overline{)63}$, quotient: 5
7. $\boxed{}\overline{)28}$, quotient: 7
8. $\boxed{}\overline{)63}$, quotient: 7
9. $\boxed{}\overline{)32}$, quotient: 8
10. $\boxed{}\overline{)72}$, quotient: 12
11. $\boxed{}\overline{)36}$, quotient: 6
12. $\boxed{}\overline{)98}$, quotient: 11
13. $\boxed{}\overline{)36}$, quotient: 4
14. $\boxed{}\overline{)54}$, quotient: 6

Lesson 5

Division Word Problems

Use division to solve the problems below.

1. Rachel bought three pairs of ballet shoes for $99. What is the cost of each pair of shoes?

2. Charlie has 21 kids in his class. If he divides the kids into 3 groups how many kids will be in each group?

3. Sara loves her dolls; she has 12 of them. If she divides them into groups of 4, how many dolls will be in each group?

4. Harry has 72 toy trucks and cars. If he divides them into groups of 8, how many cars and trucks will be in each group?

Lesson 6

2-Digit Quotients 1

Estimate	Divide the tens	Bring down the ones and repeat the steps.	The answer is: **23 r 3**
$4\overline{)95}$ with quotient 2	$4\overline{)95}$ with quotient 2 - 8 1	$4\overline{)95}$ with quotient 23 - 8↓ 15 - 12 3	Remember these steps: 1. Divide 2. Multiply 3. Subtract 4. Bring down
Take a look at the first digit. Estimate how many times 4 will go into 9 without going over the number.	4 can go into 9 twice. Multiply 4 x 2 and get 8. Subtract the 8 from 9 leaving 1.	Bring down the 5 from the one's column and repeat the steps. **The remainder is 3**	Repeat these steps until there are no more digits to bring down.

Divide these problems. Some may not have remainders.

1. $2\overline{)57}$ = 28 r 1
- 4
17
- 16
1

2. $3\overline{)72}$

3. $4\overline{)65}$

4. $3\overline{)86}$

5. $2\overline{)37}$

6. $7\overline{)93}$

7. $5\overline{)73}$

8. $7\overline{)98}$

2-Digit Quotients 2

Divide these problems. Some may not have remainders.

1. $6\overline{)98}$ **2.** $3\overline{)65}$ **3.** $2\overline{)85}$ **4.** $4\overline{)99}$

5. $3\overline{)54}$ **6.** $6\overline{)77}$ **7.** $6\overline{)97}$ **8.** $2\overline{)59}$

9. $3\overline{)76}$ **10.** $2\overline{)46}$ **11.** $6\overline{)89}$ **12.** $3\overline{)44}$

Lesson 7

Dividing 3-Digit Numbers 1

When dividing a three-digit number by a two-digit number, the quotient may have two or three digits. Here are some examples:

Estimate	Divide	Estimate	Divide
200 3)719 →	239 r2 3)719 - 6 11 - 9 29 - 27 2	70 3)235 →	78 r1 3)235 - 21 25 - 24 1
1. Divide **2.** Multiply **3.** Subtract **4.** Compare **5.** Bring down **Repeat the steps as needed**		**1.** Divide **2.** Multiply **3.** Subtract **4.** Compare **5.** Bring down **Repeat the steps as needed**	

Divide these problems. Some may not have remainders.

1. 4)987 = 246 r 3
- 8
18
-16
27
- 24
3

2. 6)297

3. 2)592

4. 3)769

5. 4)867

6. 5)934

Dividing 3-Digit Numbers 2

Divide these problems, some may not have remainders.

1. $6\overline{)987}$ **2.** $5\overline{)857}$ **3.** $4\overline{)827}$

4. $4\overline{)359}$ **5.** $9\overline{)289}$ **6.** $2\overline{)764}$ **7.** $7\overline{)357}$

8. $2\overline{)923}$ **9.** $4\overline{)577}$ **10.** $9\overline{)956}$ **11.** $5\overline{)234}$

12. $8\overline{)649}$ **13.** $7\overline{)937}$ **14.** $3\overline{)899}$ **15.** $4\overline{)521}$

Lesson 8

Averaging 1

An average is found by adding two or more quantities together and dividing by the number of quantities.

Step 1: Find the sum of the quantities ⟶ 35 + 15 + 10 = 60

Step 2: Divide by the number of quantities ⟶ 60 ÷ 3 = (20)

Work the problems out. Find the average of each set of numbers.

1. 6, 12, 15 = 11

$$\begin{array}{r} 6 \\ 12 \\ +\ 15 \\ \hline 33 \end{array} \div 3 = \textcircled{11}$$

2. 1, 13, 9, 65 = _____

3. 2, 7, 11, 12 = _____

4. 48, 23, 28 = _____

5. 2, 29, 35, 18 = _____

6. 9, 33, 17, 29 = _____

Averaging 2

Find the average of each set of numbers.
Work the problems out.

1. 10, 62, 24 = _____

2. 28, 72, 44 = _____

3. 13, 51, 87, 65 = _____

4. 25, 78, 92, 13 = _____

5. 63, 32, 72, 90, 98 = _____

6. 100, 59, 87, 33, 21 = _____

Lesson 9

Averaging Word Problems

Write out each averaging problem and solve.

1. Jamie wants to know her average test score in math class. On her 4 tests she scored 79, 86, 92 and 80. What is her average test score?

2. Steven scored 17, 16, 19, 27, 21 points in 5 games. How many points did he average?

3. Kenny is good at video games. He played the game 6 times. He scored 128, 58, 166, 164, 212 and 72. What is his average score?

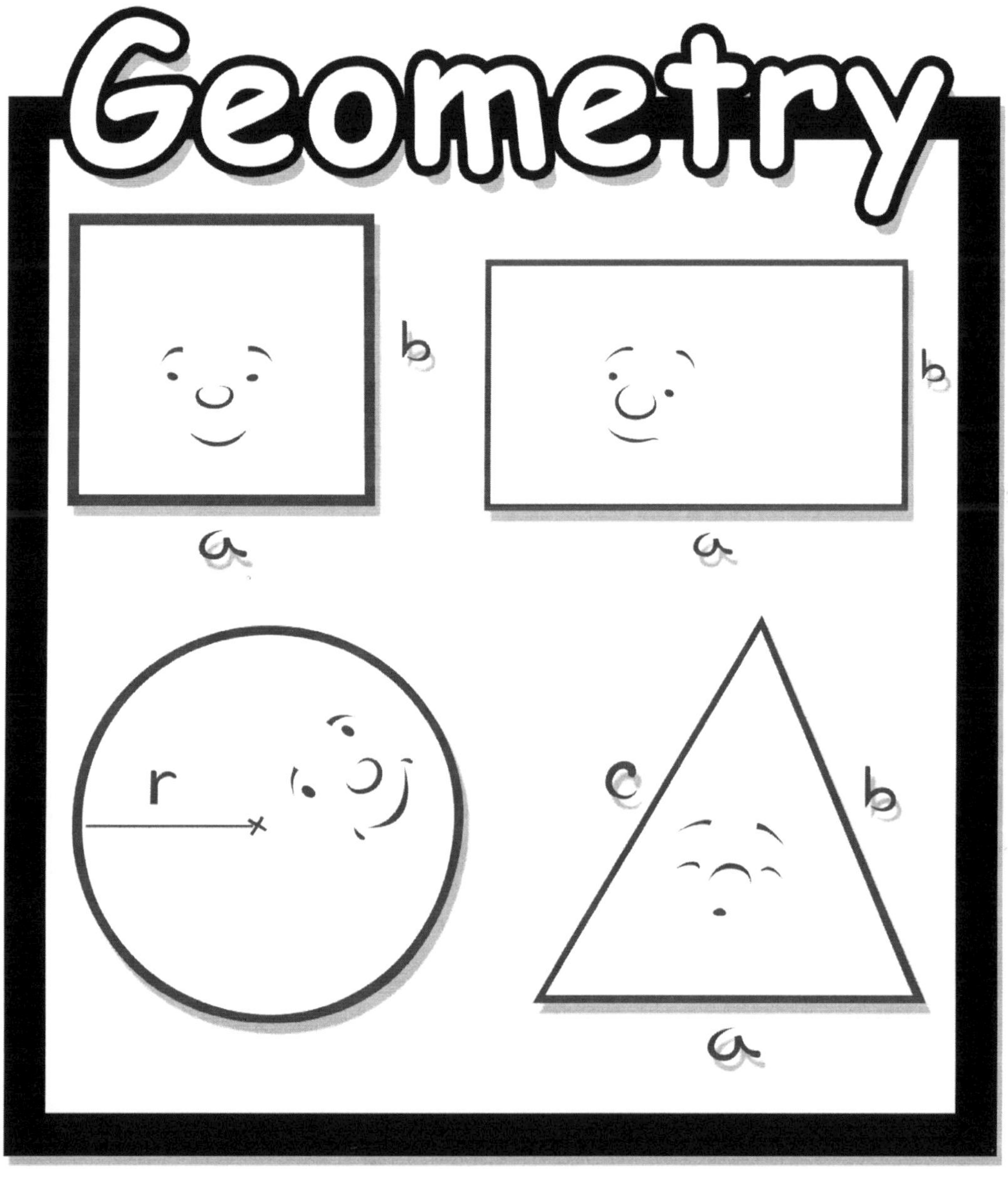
Geometry
b
a
b
a
r
c
b
a

Lesson 1

Flat Shapes

Identifying Flat Shapes

Write the number of sides in each box below.
Write the name of each shape in the blanks.

1. 

7 heptagon

2. 

3. 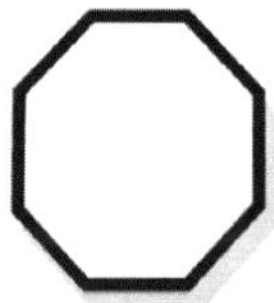

4. 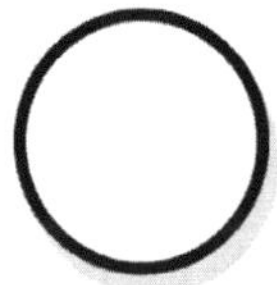

5. 

6. 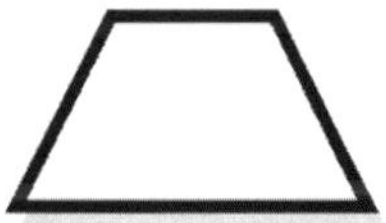

7. 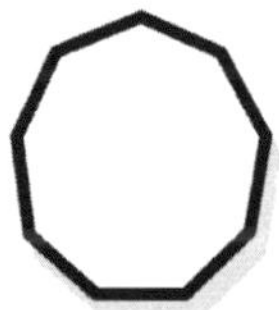

8. 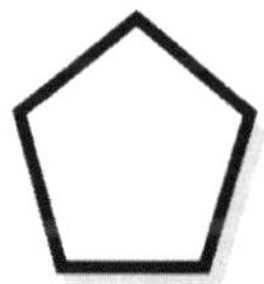

9. 

10. 

11. 

12. 

13. 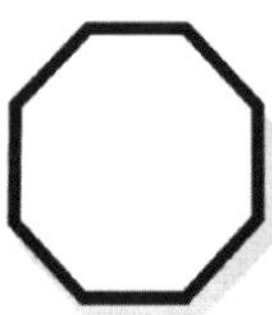

14. 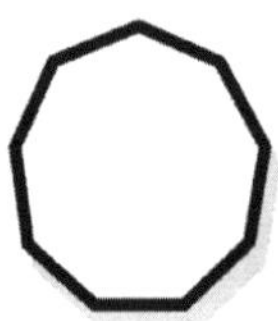

15. 

16. 

Lesson 2

Solid Shape

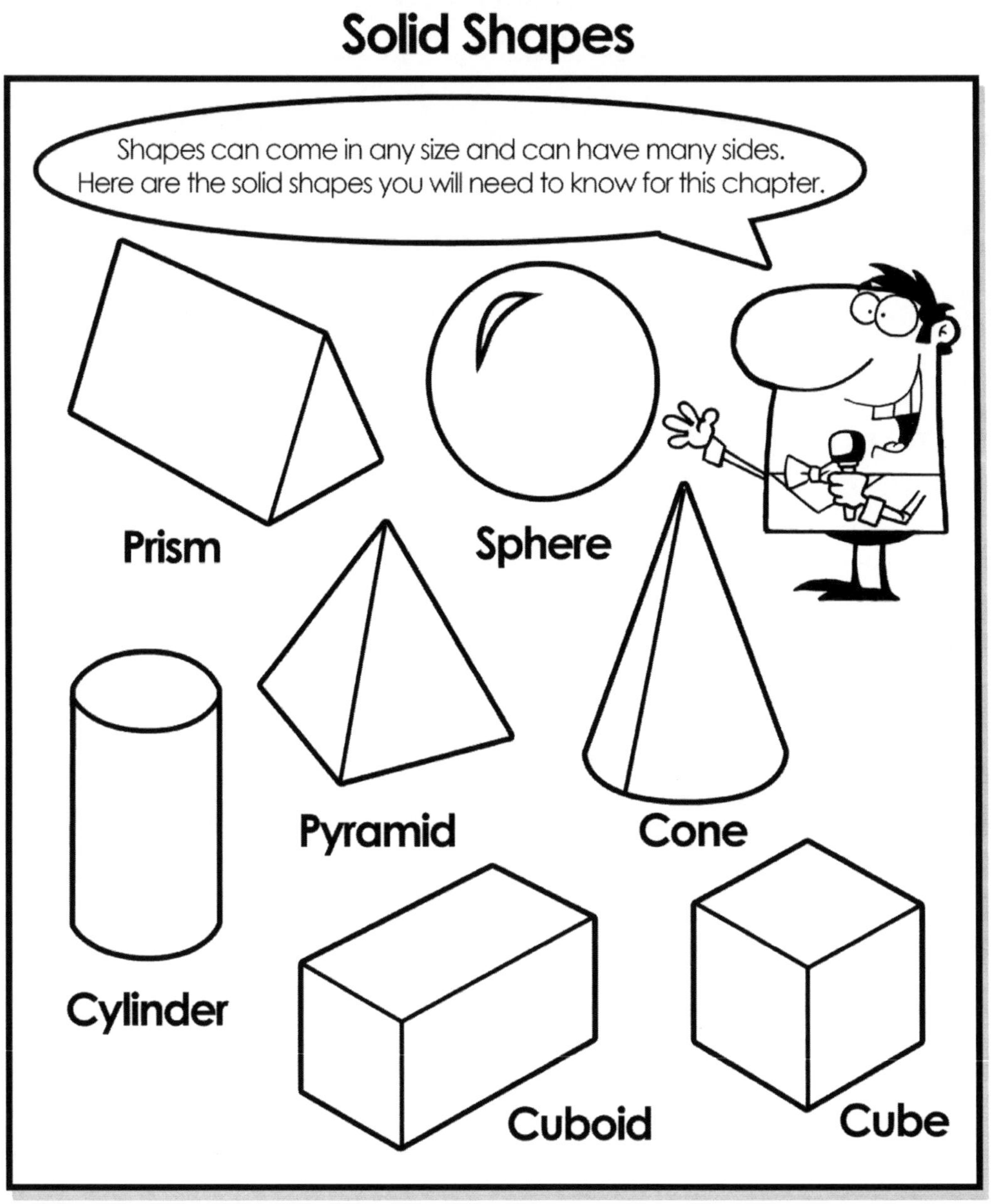

Identifying Solid Shape

Identify each shape below and write the names in the blanks.

1.
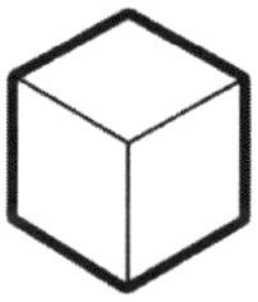
cube
______

2.
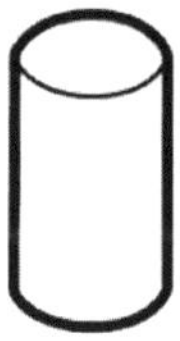
______

3.

______

4.

______

5.

______

6.
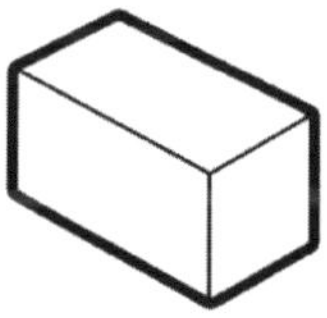
______

7.

______

8.

______

9.

______

10.
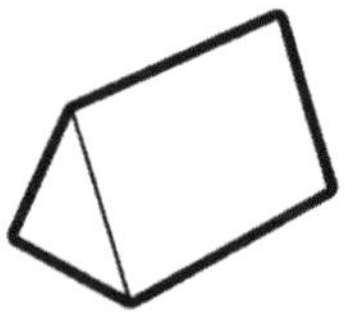
______

11.
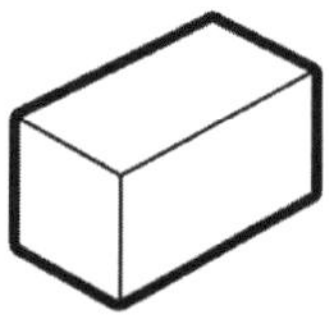
______

12.

______

13.
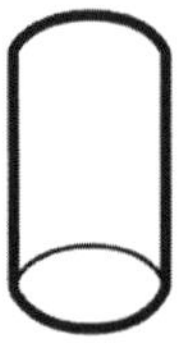
______

14.
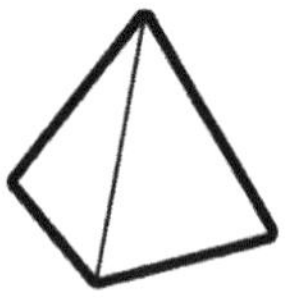
______

15.
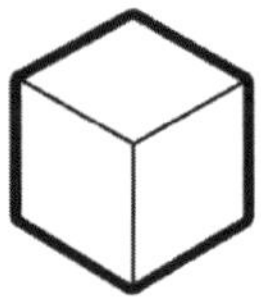
______

16.
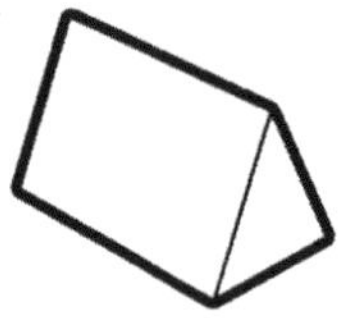
______

Lesson 3

Identifying Triangles

Triangles can come in many shapes. Here are some examples.

Equilateral	**Isosceles**	**Scalene**	**Right Angle**
All sides are equal	Two sides equal	No sides equal	Contains at least one right angle

Name each triangle as an **equilateral**, **isosceles**, **scalene** or **right** triangle.

1. 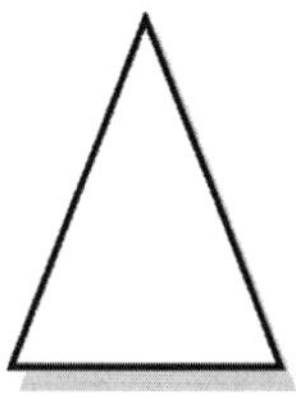 isosceles

2. 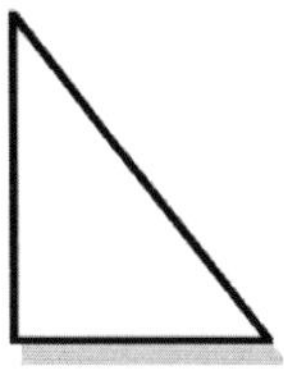 ____________

3. 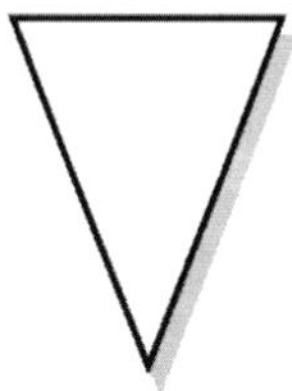 ____________

4. 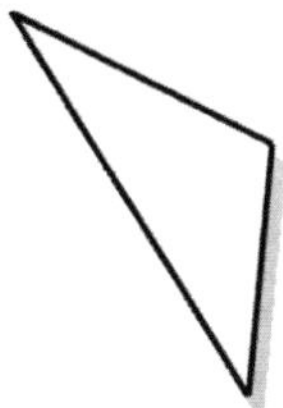 ____________

5. 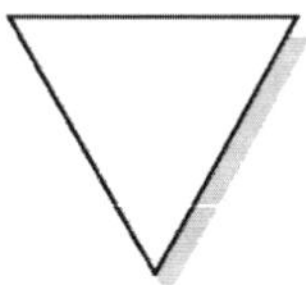 ____________

6. 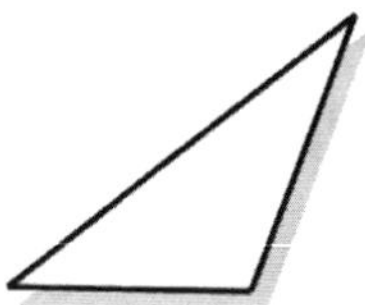 ____________

7. 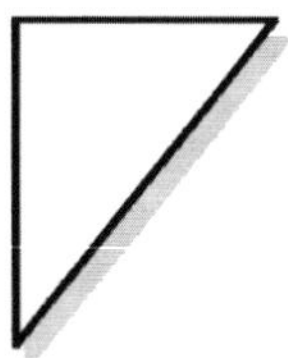 ____________

8. 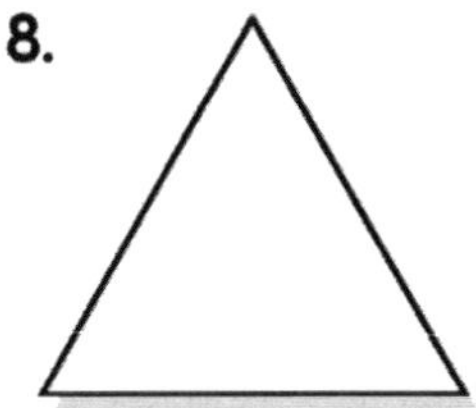 ____________

Lesson 4

Identifying Points, Lines and Rays

A **point** is an exact location in space.	A **line** is an endless straight path.	A **line segment** is a straight path between two points.	A **ray** is a part of a line, it has one endpoint and continues on in one direction.	A **vertex** is a point formed from two rays sharing a common endpoint.
				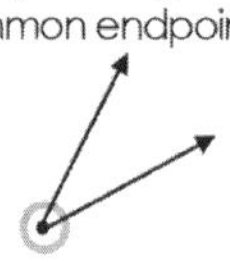

Identify each figure below.

1. 

vertex

2. 

____

3.

____

4.

____

5. 

____

6.

____

7. 

____

8.

____

9. 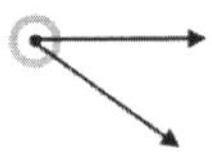

____

10. 

____

11. 

____

12. 

____

Lesson 5

Identifying Parallel and Perpendicular Lines

Intersecting lines cross each other

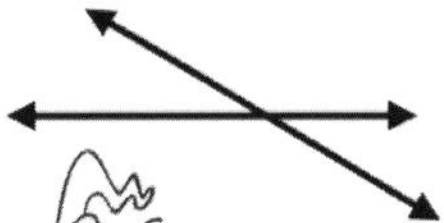

Parallel lines never intersect

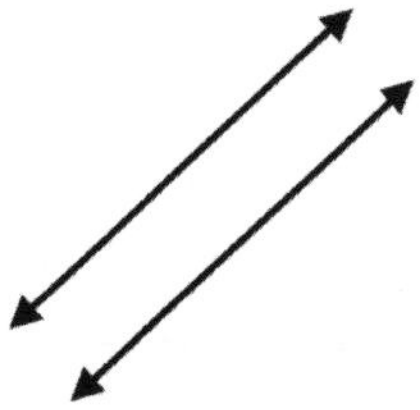

Perpendicular lines intersect to form a right angle

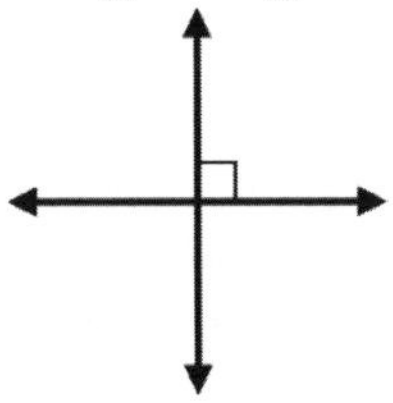

Answer if each set of lines are parallel, perpendicular or intersecting.

1. 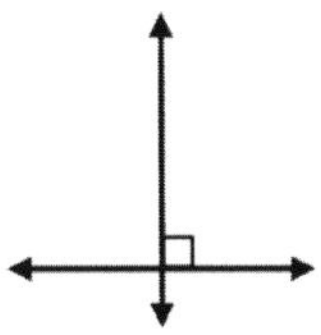

perpendicular

2. 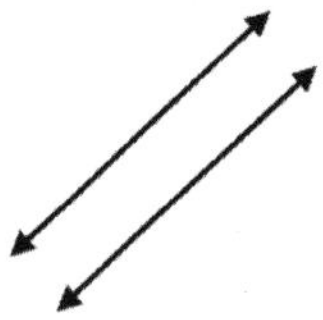

____

3. 

____

4. 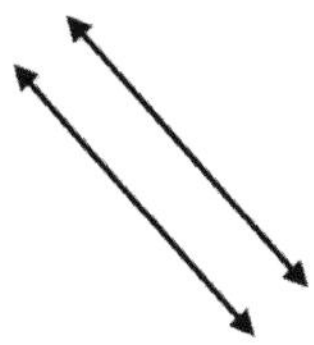

____

5. 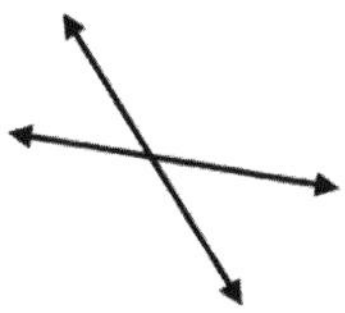

____

6. 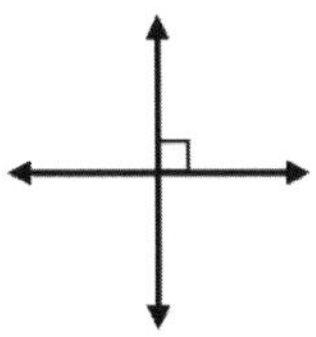

____

7. 

____

8. 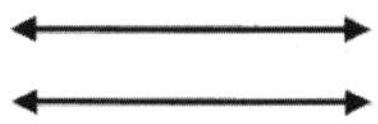

____

9. 

____

10. 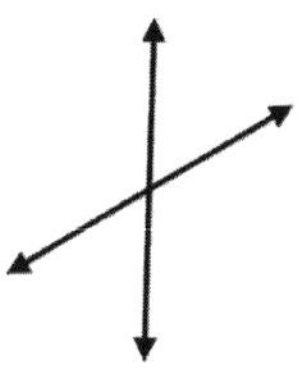

____

11. 

____

12. 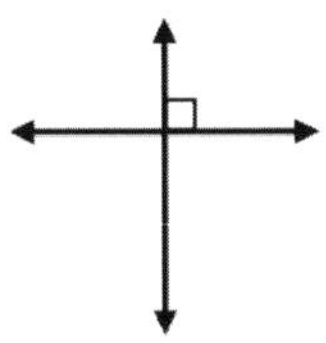

____

Lesson 6

Identifying Angles

Angles are where two lines meet.

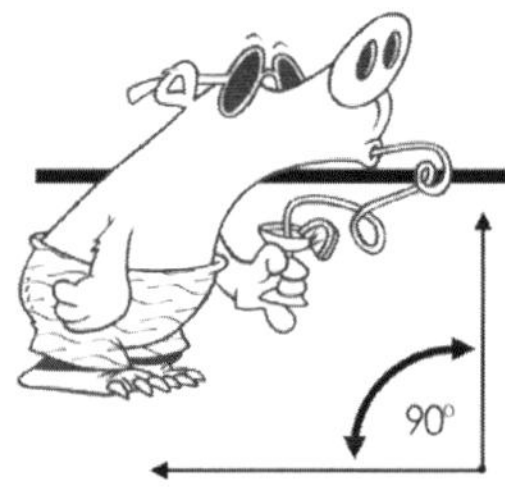

An angle that is exactly 90° is a **right angle**.

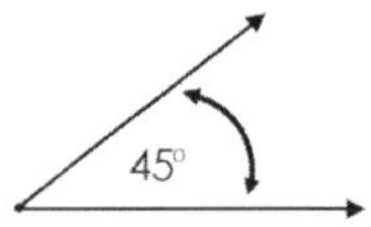

An angle that is less than 90° is an **acute angle**.

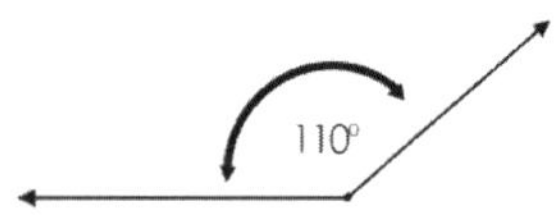

An angle that is more than 90° is an **obtuse angle**.

Identify if each angle is a **right**, **acute** or **obtuse** angle.

1. 

obtuse

2. 

____

3. 

____

4. 

____

5. 

____

6. 

____

7. 

____

8. 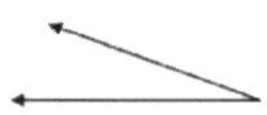

____

9. 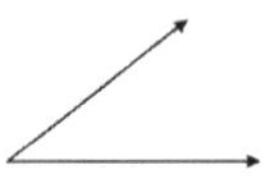

____

10. 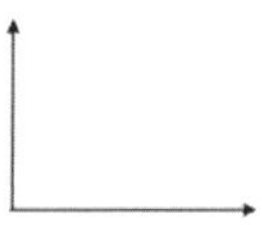

____

11. 

____

12. 

____

Lesson 7

Finding Area

Area is the measurement of a shape's surface area.
To find the **area** of a shape, multiply the length by the width.

Area = 24 ft. x 8 ft. = 192 ft.
Area = 192 sq. ft.

Find the area of each shape. Write the problem out.

1.

6 x 6 = 36 sq. in.

2.

____

3.

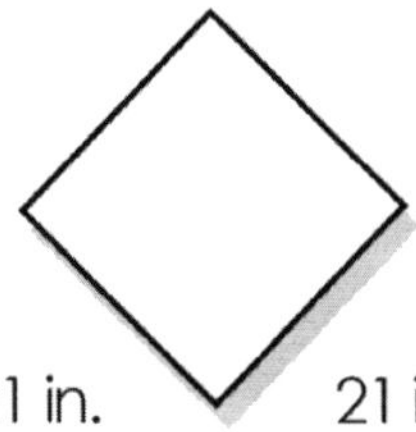

____

4.

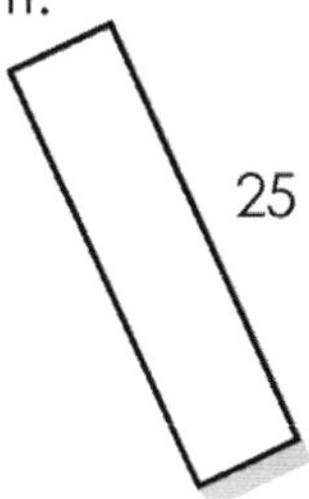

____

5.

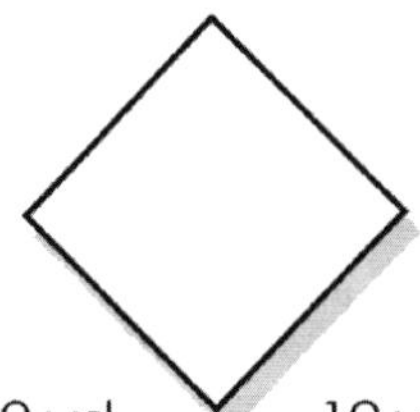

____

6.

____

Lesson 8

Finding Perimeter 1

Perimeter is the distance around an object.
Find the perimeter of each object by adding all the sides.

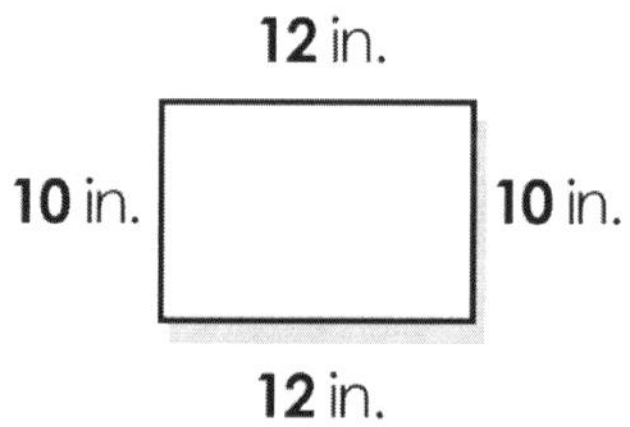

Perimeter = 12 in. + 12 in. + 10 in. + 10 in.

Perimeter = 44 in.

Find the perimeter of each shape. Write the problem out.

1.

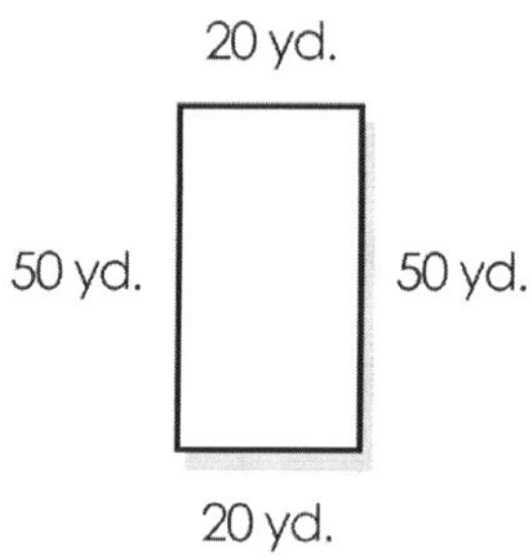

20 + 50 + 20 + 50 = 140yd.

2.

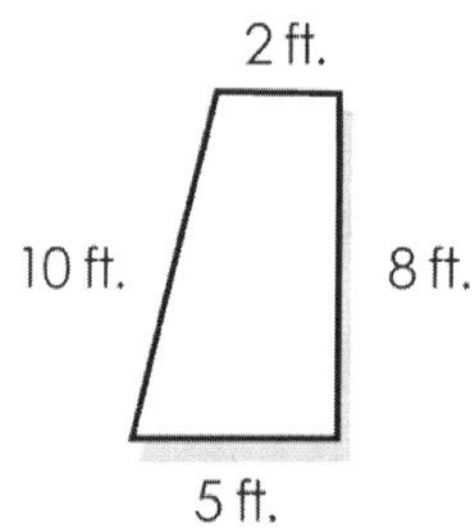

____

3.

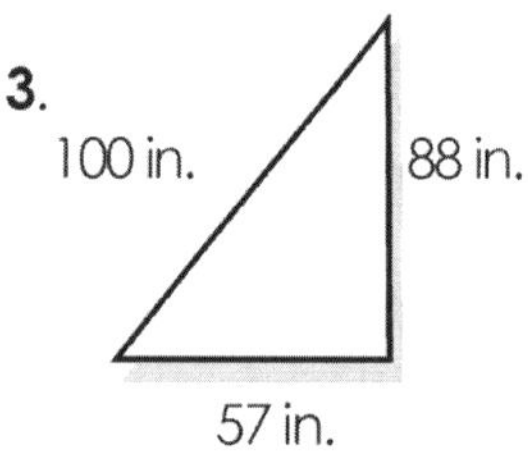

____

4.

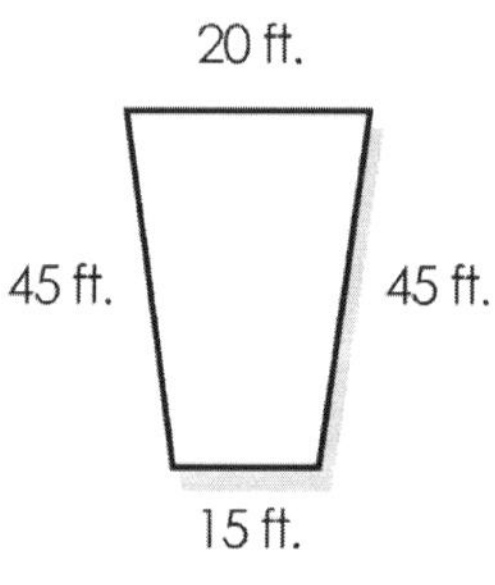

____

5.

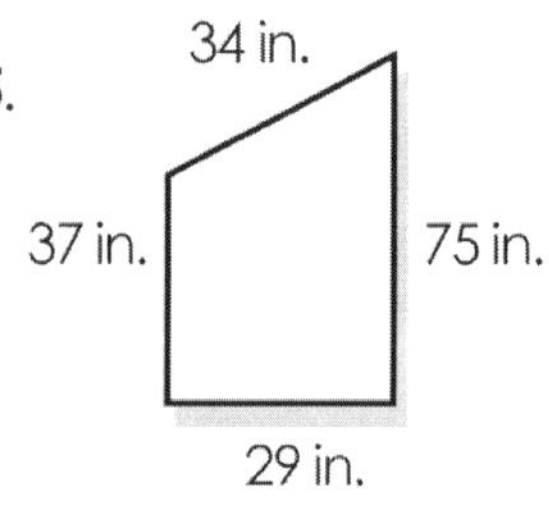

____

6.

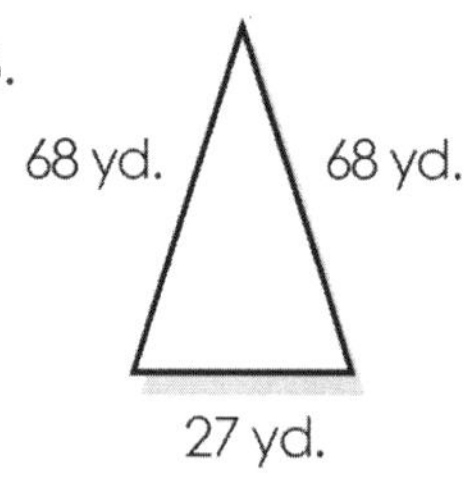

____

Finding Perimeter 2

Find the perimeter of each shape.
Write the problem out.

1.

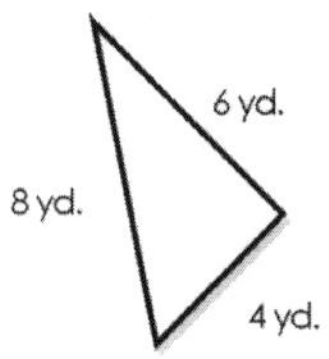

8 + 4 + 6 = 18yd.

2.

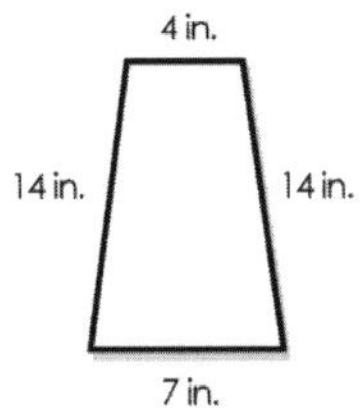

3.

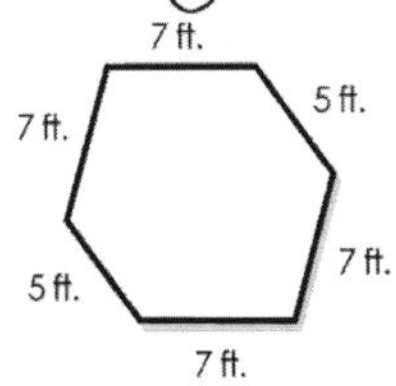

4.

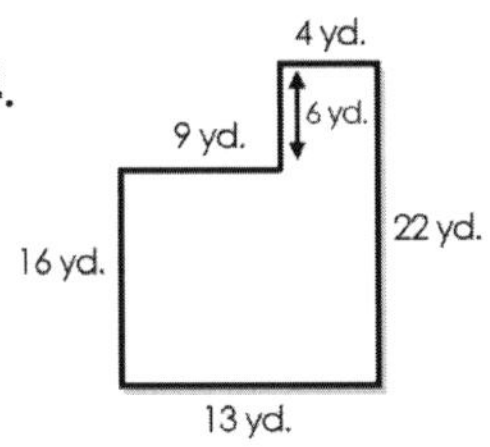

5.

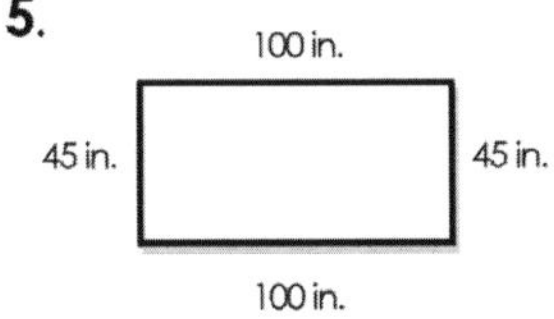

6.

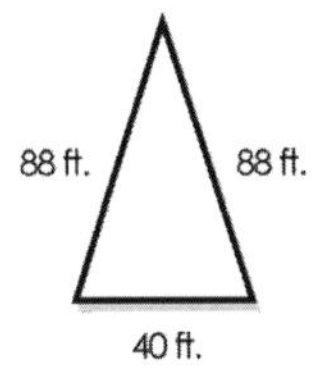

7.

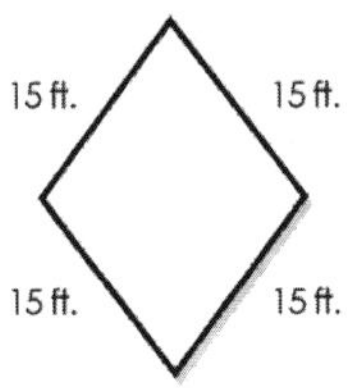

8.

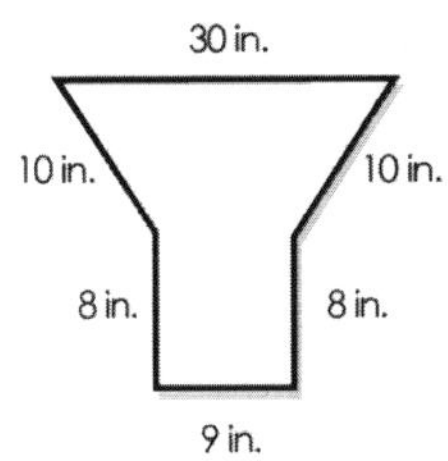

9.

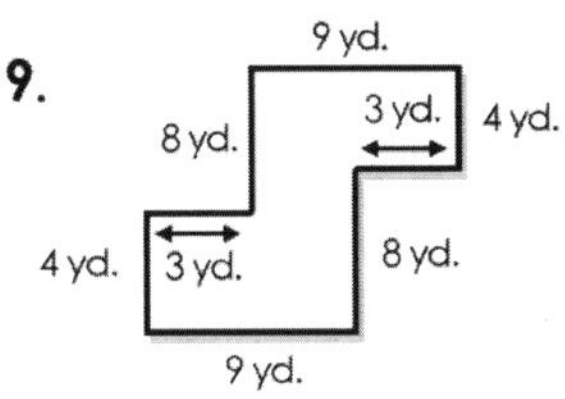

Lesson 9

Understanding Volume 1

This cube is 1 ft long, 1 ft high and 1 ft wide. It has a volume of 1 cubic foot. ($1 ft^3$).

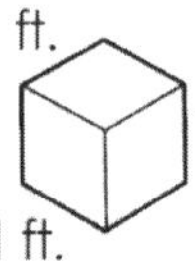

When 4 of these cubes are put together, the new shape has a volume of $4 ft^3$.

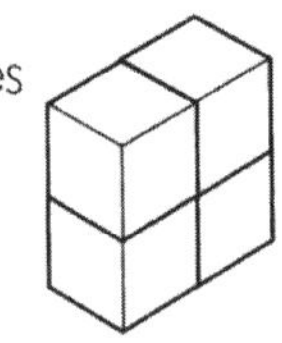

Find the volume of the shapes below.

1.

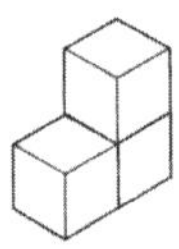

3 ft^3

2.

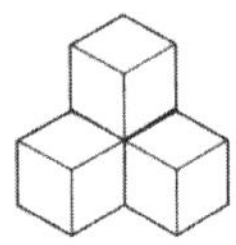

________ ft^3

3.

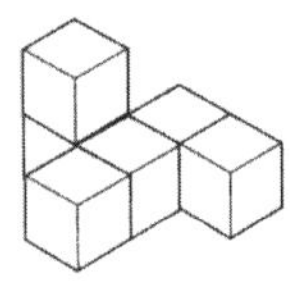

________ ft^3

4.

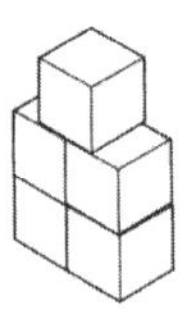

________ ft^3

5.

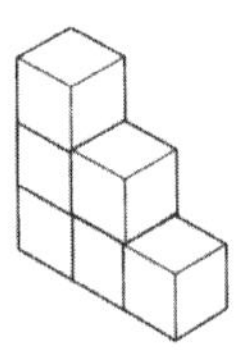

________ ft^3

6.

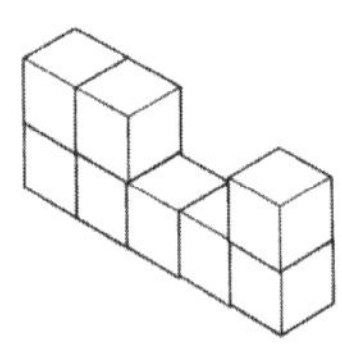

________ ft^3

7.

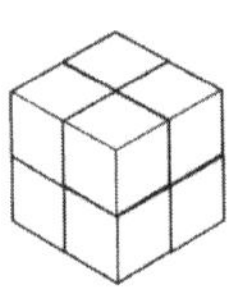

________ ft^3

8.

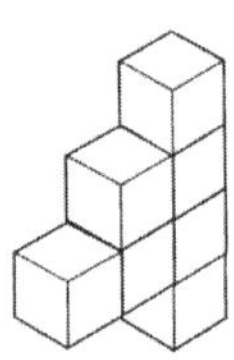

________ ft^3

9.

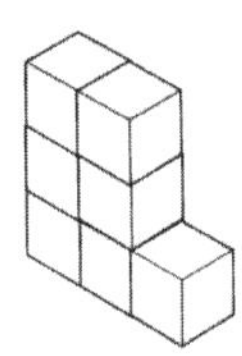

________ ft^3

Understanding Volume 2

Volume is the number of cubic units that can fit into a shape. To find volume, count the cubes or multiply length times width times height. *(L x W x H = volume)*

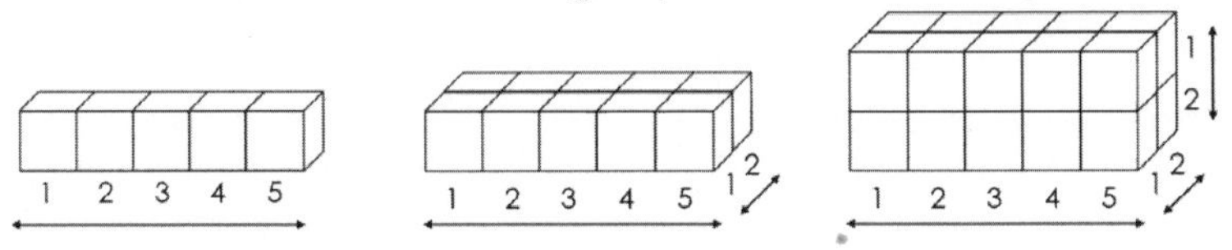

5 cubic units | 5 x 2 = 10 cubic units | 5 x 2 x 2 = 20 cubic units

Find the volume of the shapes below.

1. 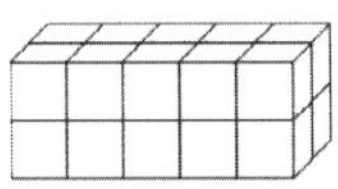

5 x 2 x 2 = 20 cubic units

2. 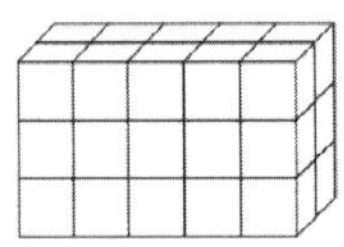

__________ cubic units

3. 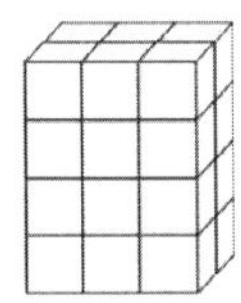

__________ cubic units

4. 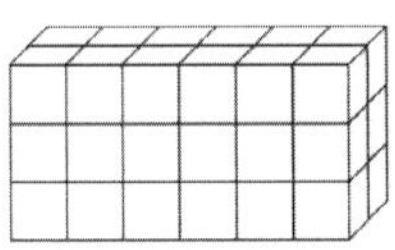

__________ cubic units

5. 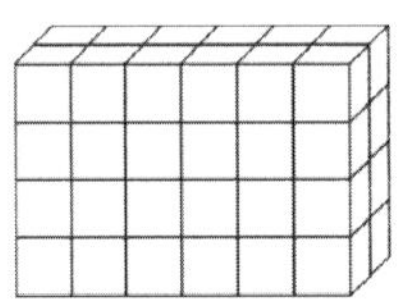

__________ cubic units

6. 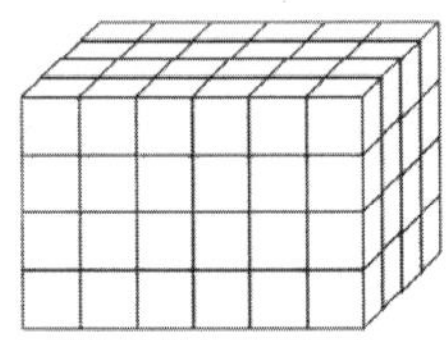

__________ cubic units

7. 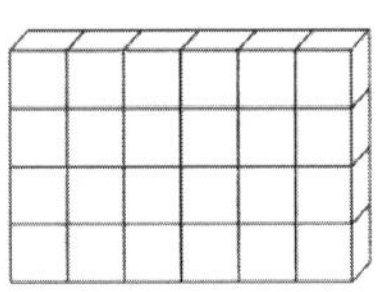

__________ cubic units

8. 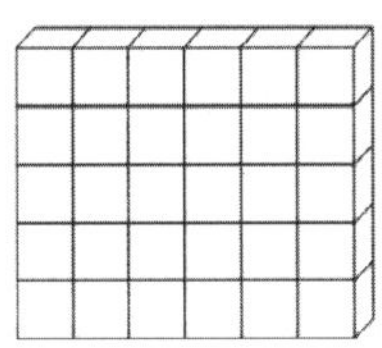

__________ cubic units

9. 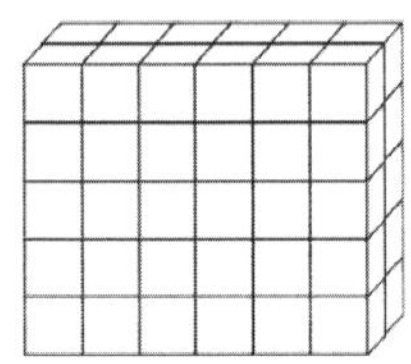

__________ cubic units

Understanding Volume 3

Volume is the number of cubic units that can fit into a shape.
To find volume, multiply length times width times height.
(L x W x H = volume)

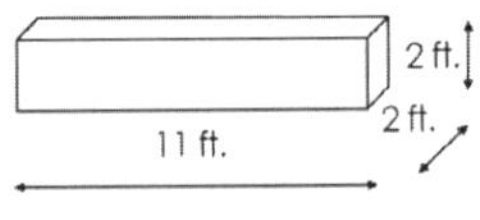

11 x 2 x 2 = 44 cubic feet

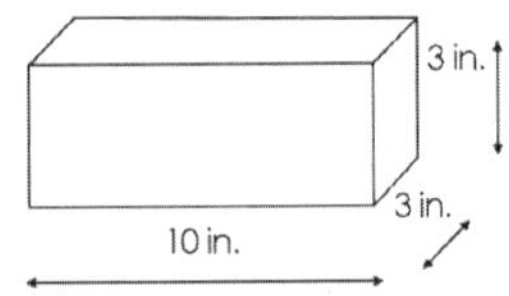

10 x 3 x 3 = 90 cubic inches

Find the volume of the shapes below.

1.

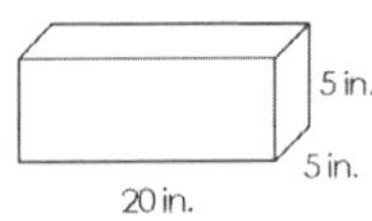

20 x 5 x 5 = 500 $in.^3$

2.

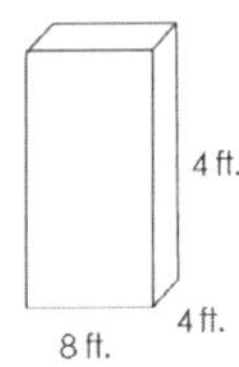

3.

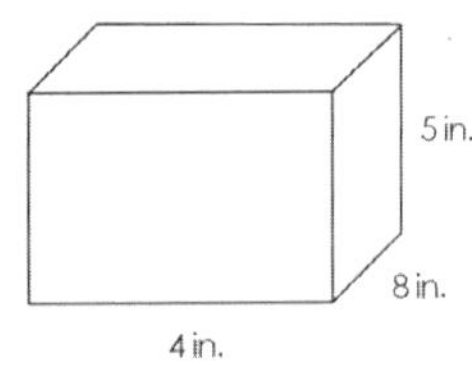

4.

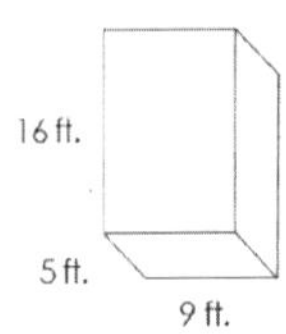

5.

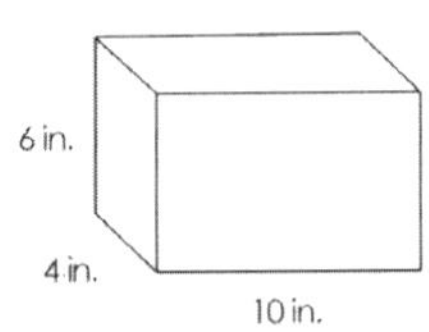

6.

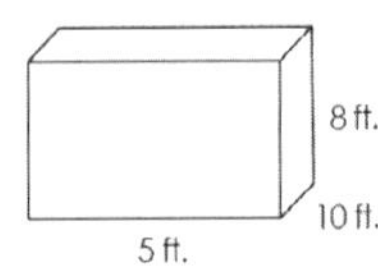

7.

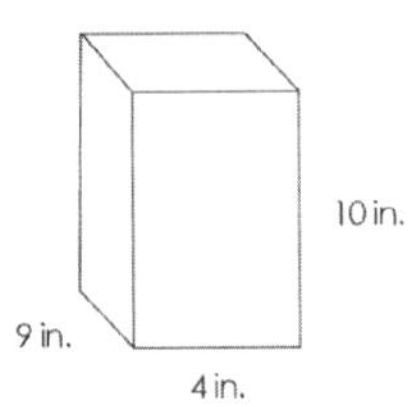

8.

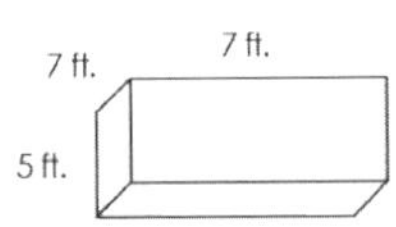

9.

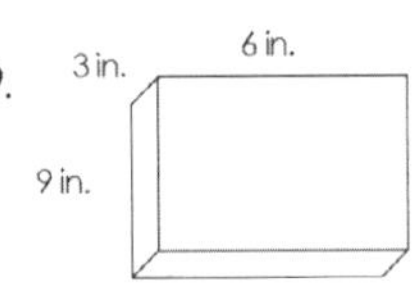

Chapter 8 - Measurements

Lesson 1

Measurement

Capacity	Length	Weight
1 gallon = 8 pints	1 foot = 12 inches	1 pound = 16 ounces
1 gallon = 4 quarts	1 yard = 3 feet	1 ton = 2000 pounds
1 gallon = 16 cups	1 yard = 36 inches	1 ton = 32000 ounces
1 gallon = 128 fluid ounces	1 mile = 5280 feet	
1 quart = 4 cups	1 mile = 1760 yards	
1 quart = 2 pints		
1 pint = 2 cups		
1 cup = 8 fluid ounces		
1 pint = 16 fluid ounces		

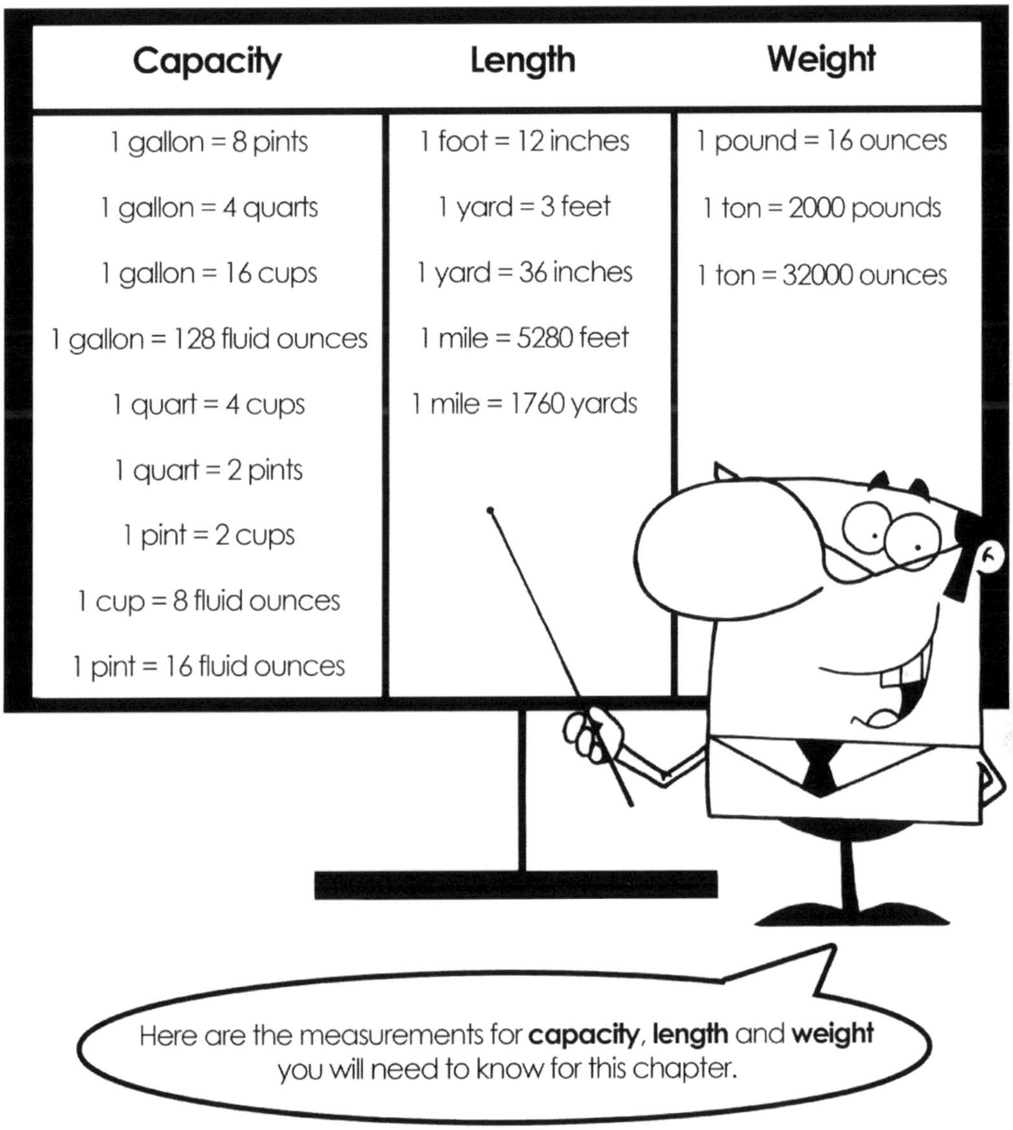

Lesson 2

Ounces, Pounds and Tons Word Problems

Circle the correct answer for each question.

1. Lilly has grown a lot over the summer. How much does she weigh now?

(60 pounds) 60 ounces 60 tons

2. Dad's new truck is very heavy; how much does it weigh?

2 pounds 2 ounces 2 tons

3. Jan needs to sell more cookies to go on the trip. How many more cookies does she need to sell?

5 pounds 5 ounces 5 tons

4. The pumpkin we grew is huge. How much does it weigh?

37 pounds 37 ounces 37 tons

Ounces, Pounds and Tons

One - half pound (lb.) = 8 ounces (oz.)
1 pound (lb.) = 16 ounces (oz.)
One - half ton (T.) = 1,000 pounds (lb.)
1 ton (T.) = 2,000 pounds (lb.)

Complete the problems below.

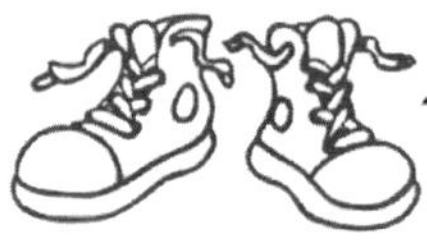

1. 48 oz. = __3__ lb.

2. 32 lb. = ______ oz.

3. 4,000 lb. = ______ T.

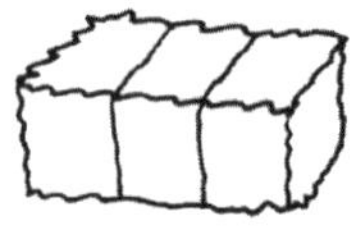

4. 80 oz. = ______ lb.

5. 2 lb. = ______ oz.

6. 8 lb. = ______ oz.

7. 3T. = ______ lb.

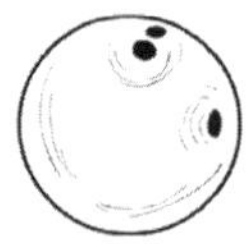

8. 6 lb. = ______ oz.

9. 16 oz. = ______ lb.

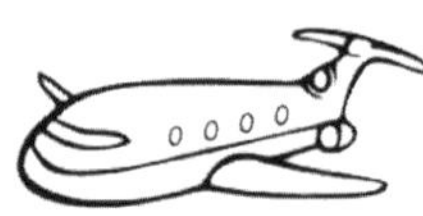

10. 12,000 lb. = ______ T.

Lesson 3

Estimating Length

Circle the best unit of measurement to estimate each item's length.

1.	Length of your foot.		Inches	Feet
2.	Length of your house.		Inches	Feet
3.	Length of your pen.		Inches	Feet
4.	Height of your dad.		Inches	Feet
5.	Length of your car.		Inches	Feet
6.	Length of your hair.		Inches	Feet

Lesson 4

Inches, Feet and Yards

12 inches = 1 foot	3 feet = 1 yard
36 inches = 1 yard	

Compare inches to feet.

Use the symbols **<**, **>**, and **=** to answer the questions below

1.	10 feet	>	100 inches	**2.**	20 inches	___	3 feet
3.	12 inches	___	1 foot	**4.**	6 feet	___	50 inches
5.	40 inches	___	3 feet	**6.**	5 feet	___	70 inches
7.	4 feet	___	48 inches	**8.**	72 inches	___	6 feet

Compare inches, feet, and yards.

Use the symbols **<**, **>**, and **=** to answer the questions below

9.	9 feet	___	32 yards	**10.**	46 inches	___	2 yards
11.	40 feet	___	3 yards	**12.**	4 yards	___	15 feet
13.	4 feet	___	100 inches	**14.**	1 foot	___	2 yards
15.	24 inches	___	1 foot	**16.**	6 yards	___	24 feet

Lesson 5

Ruler Measurement - Inches

Measure each object to the nearest $\frac{1}{2}$ or $\frac{1}{4}$ inch using the rulers below.

1. 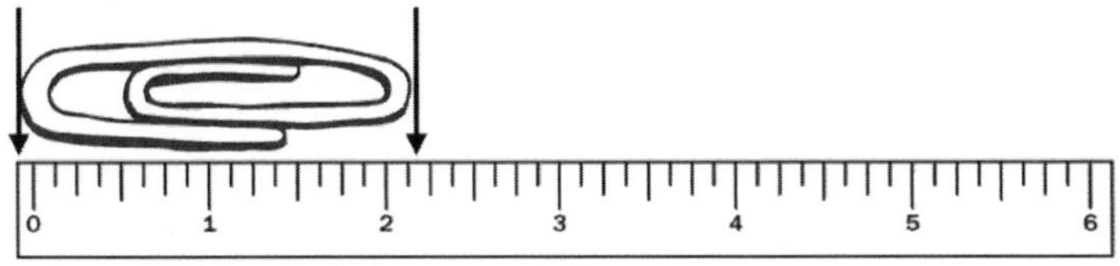

$2\frac{1}{4}$ inches

2. 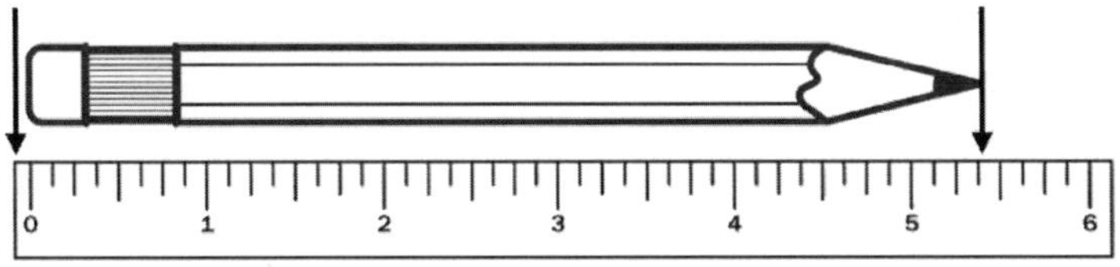

_______ inches

3. 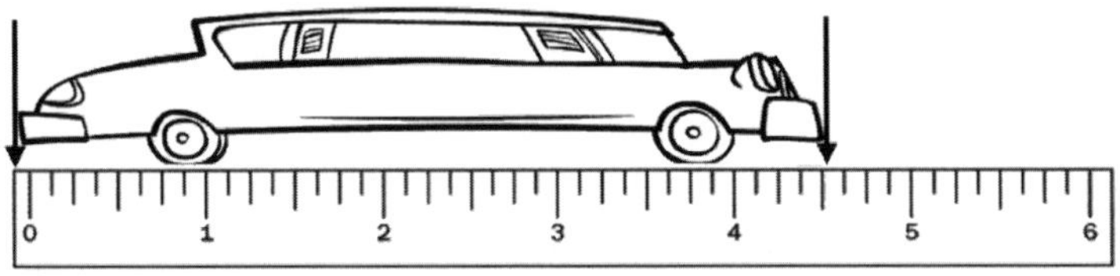

_______ inches

4. 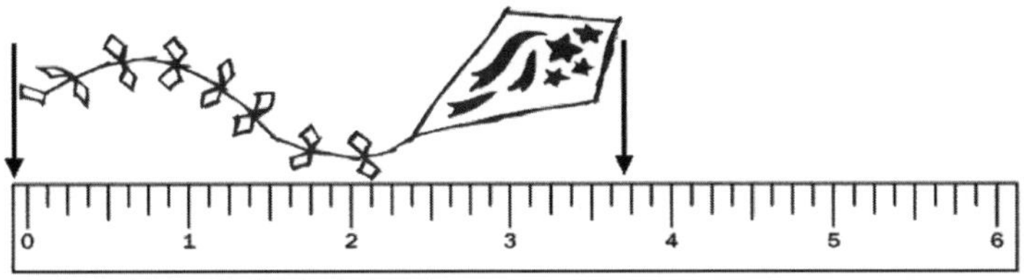

_______ inches

5. 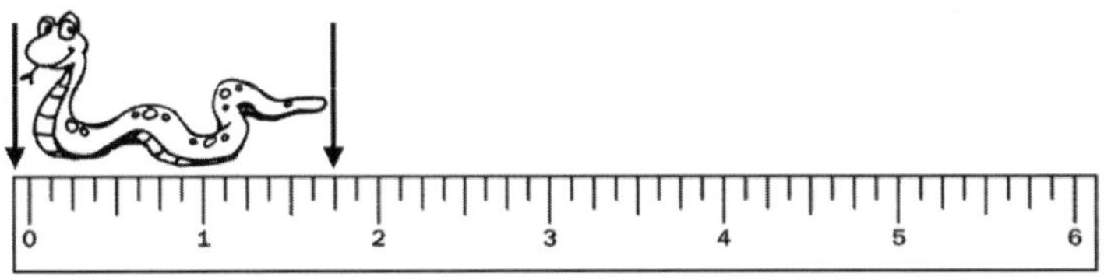

_______ inches

Ruler Measurement - Centimeters

Measure each object to the nearest centimeter.

1. 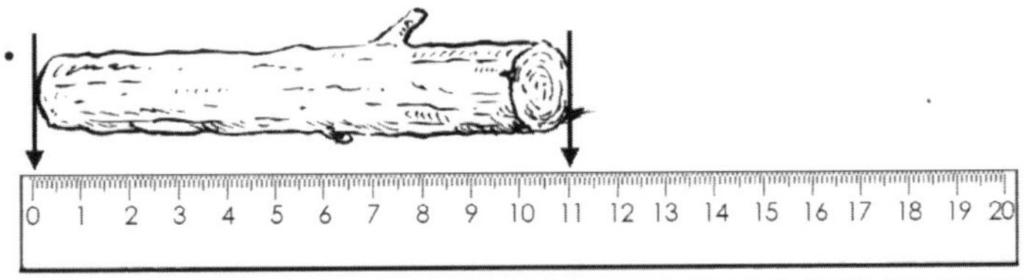

11 centimeters

2. 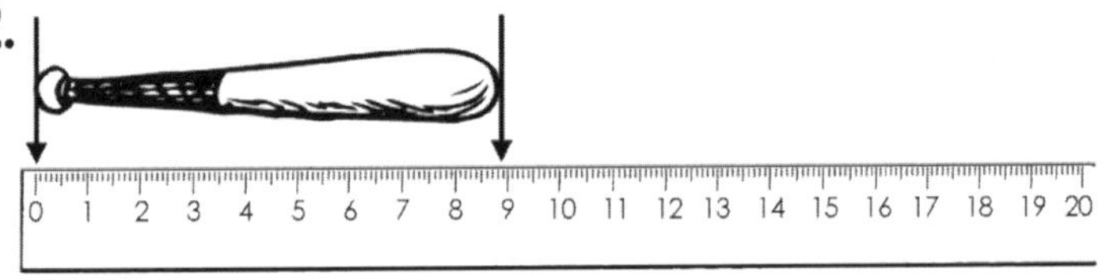

_______ centimeters

3. 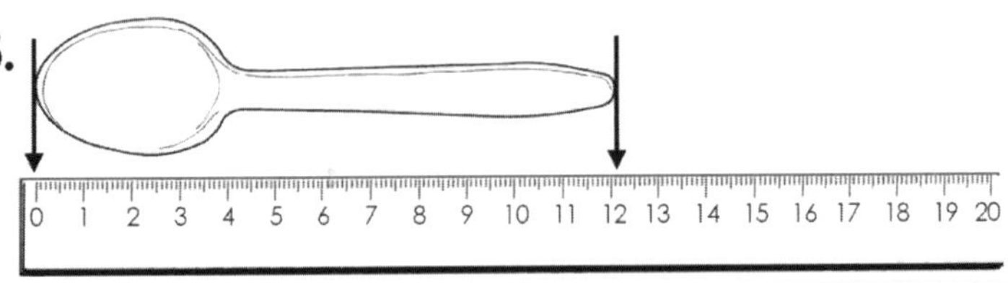

_______ centimeters

4. 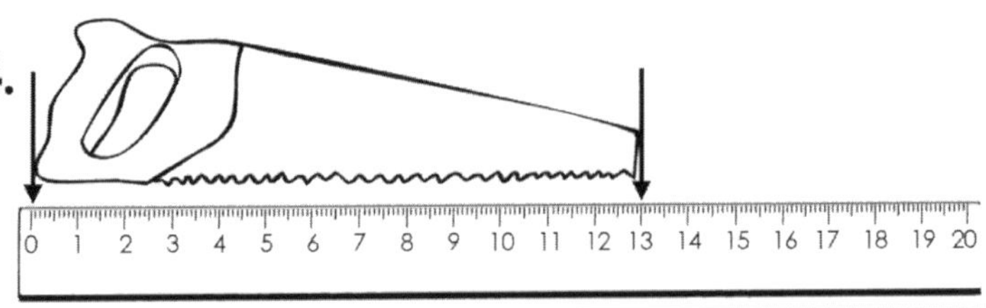

_______ centimeters

5. 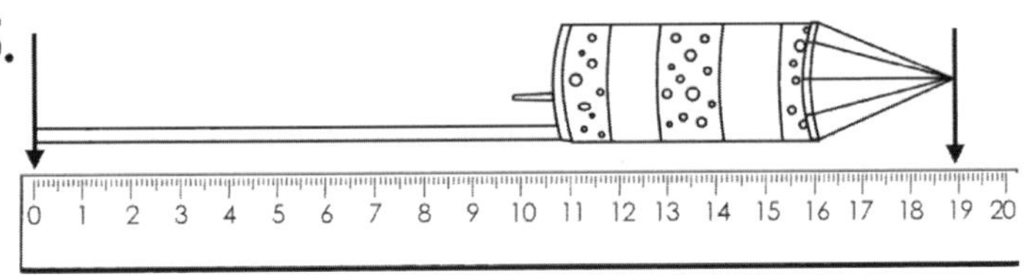

_______ centimeters

Lesson 6

Liquid Measurement 1

2 Cups = 1 Pint	2 Pints = 1 Quart	4 Quarts = 1 Gallon

Circle the number of objects to match the amount in the box.

1.

2.

3.

4.

5.

Liquid Measurement 2

1 cup (c.) = 8 ounces (oz.)

1 pint (pt.) = 2 cups (c.)

1 quart (qt.) = 2 pints (pt.)

1 quart (qt.) = 4 cups (c.)

1 gallon (gal.) = 4 quarts (qt.)

1 gallon (gal.) = 8 pints (pt.)

1 gallon (gal.) = 16 cups (c.)

Complete the problems below.

1. 14 pt. = 7 qt. **2.** 3 c. = ______ oz. **3.** 2 pt. = ______ c.

4. 16 oz. = ______ c. **5.** 2 gal. = ______ c. **6.** 2 gal. = ______ pt.

7. 32 c. = ______ gal. **8.** 8 pt. = ______ qt. **9.** 20 pt. = ______ c.

10. 13 gal. = ______ pt. **11.** 10 gal. = ______ pt. **12.** 24 oz. = ______ c.

13. 6 gal. = ______ qt. **14.** 20 pt. = ______ c. **15.** 48 c. = ______ gal.

16. 16 pt. = ______ qt. **17.** 5 c. = ______ oz. **18.** 6 pt. = ______ c.

19. 48 pt. = ______ gal. **20.** 8 pt. = ______ c. **21.** 16 pt. = ______ gal.

22. 112 oz. = ______ c. **23.** 10 qt. = ______ c. **24.** 3 gal. = ______ qt.

Liquid Measurement - Word Problems

Circle the correct answer for each question.

1. Mom is filling up the tub so I can take a bath.
How much water does she need?

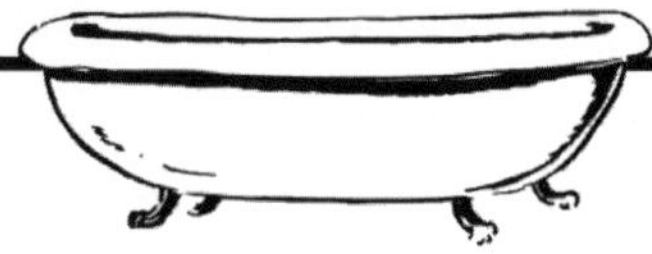

20 ounces   20 gallons

2. Danny's dog is thirsty; how much water should he put in its bowl?

3 pints   3 gallons   3 ounces

3. The car is low on gasoline. How much gas should we add?

12 cups   12 gallons   12 pints

4. How much paint should Rhea buy to paint her art project?

16 ounces   16 quarts   16 gallons

Chapter 9 - Fractions

Lesson 1

Explaining Fractions

A **fraction** names a part of a whole. It can also be used to name a part of a group or set.

Fractions are made up of two parts. The **numerator** and the **denominator**.

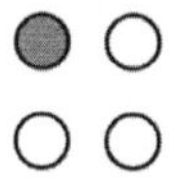 → $\frac{1}{4}$

1 ← The numerator is the number of shaded objects.

4 ← The denominator is the total number of objects.

Write what fraction of each set is shaded in.

1. 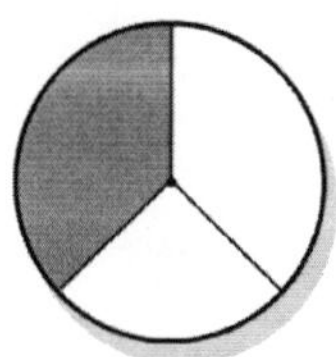 = $\frac{1}{3}$

2. 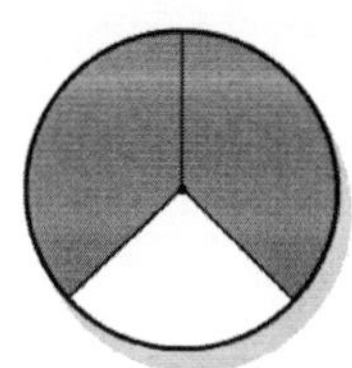 = ☐

3. 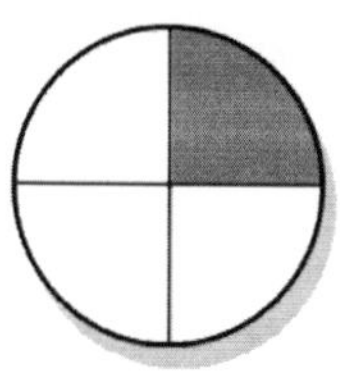 = ☐

4. 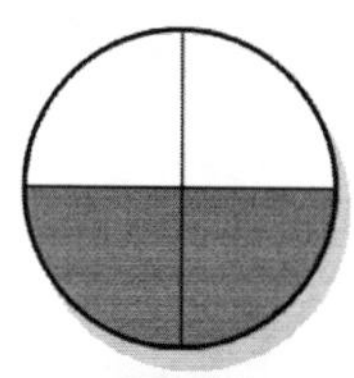 = ☐

5. 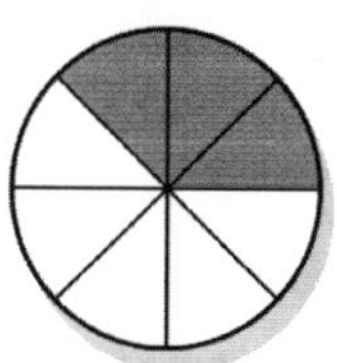 = ☐

6. 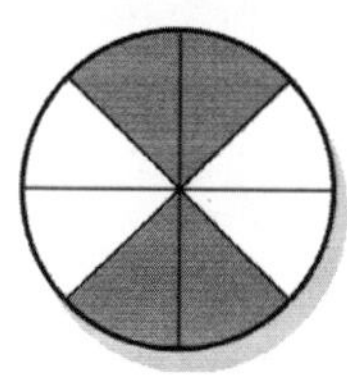 = ☐

7. 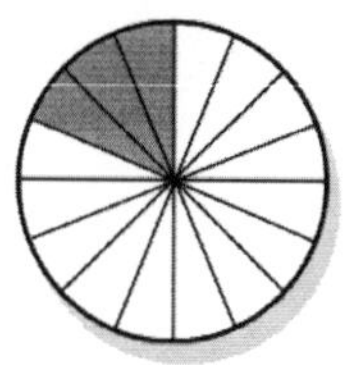 = ☐

8. 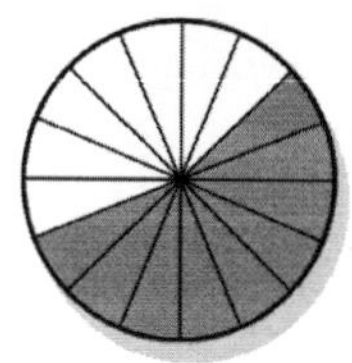 = ☐

Lesson 2

Comparing Fractions 1

- These fractions have the same denominators.
- We determine which fraction is larger by looking at the numerator.
- 6 is greater than 5. (6 > 5)

Numerator →	$6 \quad \boxed{>} \quad 5$
Denominator →	$12 \qquad 12$

$$\frac{6}{12} \ \boxed{>} \ \frac{5}{12}$$

Compare the fractions. Write >, <, or =.

1. $\frac{2}{8}\ \boxed{<}\ \frac{4}{8}$
2. $\frac{1}{5}\ \square\ \frac{4}{5}$
3. $\frac{8}{10}\ \square\ \frac{6}{10}$
4. $\frac{2}{3}\ \square\ \frac{4}{3}$
5. $\frac{6}{7}\ \square\ \frac{2}{7}$
6. $\frac{10}{15}\ \square\ \frac{2}{15}$
7. $\frac{2}{6}\ \square\ \frac{4}{6}$
8. $\frac{1}{2}\ \square\ \frac{2}{2}$
9. $\frac{5}{10}\ \square\ \frac{3}{10}$
10. $\frac{3}{8}\ \square\ \frac{4}{8}$
11. $\frac{1}{11}\ \square\ \frac{9}{11}$
12. $\frac{3}{5}\ \square\ \frac{1}{5}$
13. $\frac{1}{3}\ \square\ \frac{4}{3}$
14. $\frac{1}{4}\ \square\ \frac{3}{4}$
15. $\frac{7}{9}\ \square\ \frac{5}{9}$

Comparing Fractions 2

Compare the fractions. Write >, <, or =.

1. $\frac{3}{9} \square \frac{4}{9}$

2. $\frac{5}{8} \square \frac{7}{8}$

3. $\frac{3}{4} \square \frac{1}{4}$

4. $\frac{1}{2} \square \frac{2}{2}$

5. $\frac{7}{9} \square \frac{5}{9}$

6. $\frac{6}{40} \square \frac{16}{40}$

7. $\frac{10}{13} \square \frac{12}{13}$

8. $\frac{6}{7} \square \frac{5}{7}$

9. $\frac{9}{16} \square \frac{2}{16}$

10. $\frac{10}{11} \square \frac{2}{11}$

11. $\frac{2}{3} \square \frac{2}{3}$

12. $\frac{25}{52} \square \frac{4}{52}$

13. $\frac{60}{78} \square \frac{9}{78}$

14. $\frac{1}{10} \square \frac{2}{10}$

15. $\frac{2}{3} \square \frac{4}{3}$

16. $\frac{1}{12} \square \frac{2}{12}$

17. $\frac{1}{9} \square \frac{2}{9}$

18. $\frac{23}{29} \square \frac{4}{29}$

19. $\frac{4}{7} \square \frac{6}{7}$

20. $\frac{111}{12} \square \frac{12}{12}$

Lesson 3

Ordering Fractions

Write these fractions in order from least to greatest.

1. $1\frac{6}{10}$, $2\frac{3}{10}$, $1\frac{1}{10}$, $2\frac{1}{10}$ $1\frac{1}{10}$, $1\frac{6}{10}$, $2\frac{1}{10}$, $2\frac{3}{10}$

2. $4\frac{4}{8}$, $9\frac{6}{8}$, $6\frac{2}{8}$, $9\frac{3}{8}$

3. $6\frac{1}{4}$, $7\frac{1}{4}$, $6\frac{2}{4}$, $7\frac{3}{4}$

4. $8\frac{1}{9}$, $9\frac{1}{9}$, $8\frac{2}{9}$, $8\frac{3}{9}$

5. $3\frac{8}{12}$, $3\frac{1}{12}$, $1\frac{1}{12}$, $2\frac{3}{12}$

6. $5\frac{3}{54}$, $5\frac{2}{54}$, $5\frac{1}{54}$, $5\frac{7}{54}$

Lesson 4

Adding Fractions with Common Denominators 1

To add fractions with common denominators, just add the numerators. The denominators will remain the same.

Numerators → / Common Denominators →	$\frac{2}{9} + \frac{3}{9} = \frac{2+3}{9} = \frac{5}{9}$

Add the fractions below.

1. $\frac{1}{5} + \frac{3}{5} = \frac{4}{5}$

2. $\frac{5}{10} + \frac{3}{10} =$ ____

3. $\frac{3}{6} + \frac{2}{6} =$ ____

4. $\frac{7}{12} + \frac{3}{12} =$ ____

5. $\frac{4}{9} + \frac{4}{9} =$ ____

6. $\frac{6}{14} + \frac{2}{14} =$ ____

7. $\frac{3}{7} + \frac{2}{7} =$ ____

8. $\frac{1}{4} + \frac{2}{4} =$ ____

9. $\frac{2}{6} + \frac{3}{6} =$ ____

10. $\frac{4}{8} + \frac{3}{8} =$ ____

11. $\frac{6}{11} + \frac{3}{11} =$ ____

12. $\frac{7}{15} + \frac{5}{15} =$ ____

13. $\frac{3}{14} + \frac{9}{14} =$ ____

14. $\frac{1}{3} + \frac{1}{3} =$ ____

15. $\frac{2}{8} + \frac{4}{8} =$ ____

16. $\frac{3}{5} + \frac{1}{5} =$ ____

17. $\frac{9}{13} + \frac{2}{13} =$ ____

18. $\frac{1}{10} + \frac{6}{10} =$ ____

Adding Fractions with Common Denominators 2

To add fractions with common denominators, just add the numerators. The denominators will remain the same.

Numerators →	$\frac{2}{9} + \frac{3}{9} = \frac{2+3}{9} = \frac{5}{9}$
Common Denominators →	

Add the fractions below.

1. $\frac{2}{5} + \frac{1}{5} + \frac{1}{5} =$ ____
2. $\frac{15}{59} + \frac{3}{59} + \frac{9}{59} =$ ____
3. $\frac{4}{7} + \frac{1}{7} + \frac{2}{7} =$ ____
4. $\frac{6}{13} + \frac{2}{13} + \frac{1}{13} =$ ____
5. $\frac{4}{15} + \frac{4}{15} + \frac{3}{15} =$ ____
6. $\frac{44}{209} + \frac{19}{209} + \frac{7}{209} =$ ____
7. $\frac{6}{22} + \frac{1}{22} + \frac{9}{22} =$ ____
8. $\frac{4}{33} + \frac{1}{33} + \frac{16}{33} =$ ____
9. $\frac{3}{45} + \frac{10}{45} + \frac{11}{45} =$ ____
10. $\frac{63}{138} + \frac{23}{138} + \frac{18}{138} =$ ____
11. $\frac{1}{6} + \frac{2}{6} + \frac{1}{6} =$ ____
12. $\frac{3}{10} + \frac{3}{10} + \frac{1}{10} =$ ____

Lesson 5

Subtracting Fractions with Common Denominators 1

To subtract fractions with common denominators, just subtract the numerators. The denominators will remain the same.

Numerators →	$\frac{9}{10} - \frac{4}{10} = \frac{9-4}{10} = \frac{5}{10}$
Common Denominators →	

Subtract the fractions below.

1. $\frac{7}{15} - \frac{3}{15} = \frac{4}{15}$ **2.** $\frac{7}{9} - \frac{2}{9} =$ ____ **3.** $\frac{12}{14} - \frac{7}{14} =$ ____

4. $\frac{8}{8} - \frac{6}{8} =$ ____ **5.** $\frac{28}{39} - \frac{19}{39} =$ ____ **6.** $\frac{24}{39} - \frac{11}{39} =$ ____

7. $\frac{9}{10} - \frac{2}{10} =$ ____ **8.** $\frac{13}{15} - \frac{9}{15} =$ ____ **9.** $\frac{13}{16} - \frac{3}{16} =$ ____

10. $\frac{6}{7} - \frac{4}{7} =$ ____ **11.** $\frac{10}{26} - \frac{8}{26} =$ ____ **12.** $\frac{60}{62} - \frac{41}{62} =$ ____

13. $\frac{19}{24} - \frac{10}{24} =$ ____ **14.** $\frac{46}{54} - \frac{17}{54} =$ ____ **15.** $\frac{98}{98} - \frac{15}{98} =$ ____

Subtracting Fractions with Common Denominators 2

To subtract fractions with common denominators, just subtract the numerators. The denominators will remain the same.

Numerators → / Common Denominators →	$\frac{9}{10} - \frac{4}{10} = \frac{9-4}{10} = \frac{5}{10}$

Subtract the fractions below.

1. $\frac{23}{44} - \frac{9}{44} =$ ____

2. $\frac{6}{10} - \frac{4}{10} =$ ____

3. $\frac{30}{63} - \frac{19}{63} =$ ____

4. $\frac{45}{90} - \frac{42}{90} =$ ____

5. $\frac{12}{12} - \frac{6}{12} =$ ____

6. $\frac{28}{30} - \frac{8}{30} =$ ____

7. $\frac{4}{7} - \frac{1}{7} =$ ____

8. $\frac{15}{24} - \frac{6}{24} =$ ____

9. $\frac{45}{98} - \frac{31}{98} =$ ____

10. $\frac{5}{10} - \frac{2}{10} =$ ____

11. $\frac{5}{15} - \frac{3}{15} =$ ____

12. $\frac{8}{12} - \frac{3}{12} =$ ____

13. $\frac{20}{34} - \frac{19}{34} =$ ____

14. $\frac{6}{8} - \frac{3}{8} =$ ____

15. $\frac{14}{23} - \frac{7}{23} =$ ____

Lesson 6

Adding Mixed Numbers with Common Denominators

A **mixed number** is a number written as a whole number and a fraction.

When adding mixed numbers with common denominators, add the whole numbers first, then add the numerators. The denominators will remain the same.

$$1\frac{2}{4} + 5\frac{1}{4} = 6\frac{3}{4}$$

← Numerator

← Denominator

Add the mixed numbers below.

1. $5\frac{3}{8} + 3\frac{2}{8} = 8\frac{5}{8}$

2. $2\frac{2}{5} + 1\frac{2}{5}$

3. $9\frac{3}{10} + 3\frac{4}{10}$

4. $2\frac{6}{15} + 2\frac{4}{15}$

5. $4\frac{9}{21} + 5\frac{5}{21}$

6. $7\frac{20}{42} + 6\frac{14}{42}$

7. $13\frac{7}{9} + 3\frac{1}{9}$

8. $12\frac{6}{29} + 11\frac{9}{29}$

Lesson 7

Subtracting Mixed Numbers with Common Denominators

A **mixed number** is a number written as a whole number and a fraction.

When subtracting mixed numbers with common denominators, subtract the whole numbers first, then subtract the numerators. The denominators will remain the same.

$$9\frac{5}{6} - 4\frac{2}{6} = 5\frac{3}{6}$$

← **Numerator**

← **Denominator**

Subtract the mixed numbers below.

1. $6\frac{3}{4} - 4\frac{1}{4} = 2\frac{2}{4}$

2. $8\frac{4}{6} - 3\frac{2}{6}$

3. $5\frac{8}{9} - 2\frac{7}{9}$

4. $9\frac{11}{13} - 8\frac{9}{13}$

5. $32\frac{15}{21} - 18\frac{5}{21}$

6. $12\frac{7}{30} - 2\frac{2}{30}$

7. $17\frac{20}{26} - 11\frac{12}{26}$

8. $25\frac{13}{17} - 18\frac{8}{17}$

Lesson 8

Reducing Fractions 1

- Reducing (or simplifying) fractions means reducing a fraction to the lowest possible terms.
  - To do this, find a number that both the numerator and the denominator of the fraction are divisible by. Use that number as the numerator and denominator of a new fraction equal to one. Then divide the fractions.

Example 1:	Example 2:
$\frac{15}{20} \div \frac{5}{5} = \frac{3}{4}$ $\frac{15}{20} = \left[\frac{3}{4}\right]$	$\frac{3}{9} \div \frac{3}{3} = \frac{1}{3}$ $\frac{3}{9} = \left[\frac{1}{3}\right]$

Write the problems out and reduce the fractions below.

1. $\frac{5}{15} \div \frac{3}{3} = \frac{1}{3}$

2. $\frac{4}{12} \div \frac{\_\_\_}{\_\_\_} = \frac{\_\_\_}{\_\_\_}$

3. $\frac{6}{15} \div \frac{\_\_\_}{\_\_\_} = \frac{\_\_\_}{\_\_\_}$

4. $\frac{8}{10} \div \frac{\_\_\_}{\_\_\_} = \frac{\_\_\_}{\_\_\_}$

5. $\frac{10}{25} \div \frac{\_\_\_}{\_\_\_} = \frac{\_\_\_}{\_\_\_}$

6. $\frac{20}{25} \div \frac{\_\_\_}{\_\_\_} = \frac{\_\_\_}{\_\_\_}$

Reducing Fractions 2

- Reducing (or simplifying) fractions means reducing a fraction to the lowest possible terms.
  - To do this, find a number that both the numerator and the denominator of the fraction are divisible by. Use that number as the numerator and denominator of a new fraction equal to one. Then divide the fractions.

Write the problems out and reduce the fractions below.

1. $\frac{9}{18} \div \frac{\_\_\_}{\_\_\_} = \frac{\_\_\_}{\_\_\_}$

2. $\frac{6}{28} \div \frac{\_\_\_}{\_\_\_} = \frac{\_\_\_}{\_\_\_}$

3. $\frac{15}{18} \div \frac{\_\_\_}{\_\_\_} = \frac{\_\_\_}{\_\_\_}$

4. $\frac{12}{16} \div \frac{\_\_\_}{\_\_\_} = \frac{\_\_\_}{\_\_\_}$

5. $\frac{18}{36} \div \frac{\_\_\_}{\_\_\_} = \frac{\_\_\_}{\_\_\_}$

6. $\frac{24}{75} \div \frac{\_\_\_}{\_\_\_} = \frac{\_\_\_}{\_\_\_}$

7. $\frac{7}{49} \div \frac{\_\_\_}{\_\_\_} = \frac{\_\_\_}{\_\_\_}$

8. $\frac{27}{81} \div \frac{\_\_\_}{\_\_\_} = \frac{\_\_\_}{\_\_\_}$

Practice Test #1

Practice Questions

1. Which statement is **false**?
   a. 7 pens of 3 cattle is 20 cattle.
   b. 8 pens of 3 cattle is 24 cattle.
   c. 3 containers filled with 8 pencils is 24 pencils.
   d. 3 containers filled with 7 pencils is 21 pencils.

2. Johnny just spent $4.50 on 18 erasers. How much does one eraser cost?
   a. $0.20
   b. $0.25
   c. $0.30
   d. $0.35

3. Raquel has 36 stamps. She groups the stamps into 9 equal groups. She then adds two more stamps to each group. If she gives 4 stamps to each of her 13 friends, how many stamps will she have left?
   a. 0
   b. 1
   c. 2
   d. 3

4. The numbers 4, 6, and 10 are all factors of which number?
   a. 12
   b. 24
   c. 60
   d. 80

5. Which pattern of numbers describes the number of line segments needed in the shape pattern listed below?

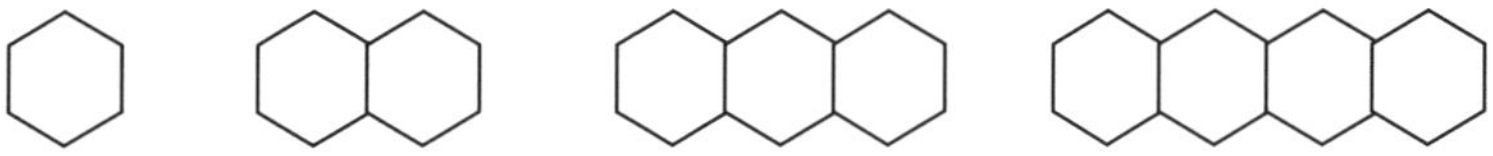

a. 1, 2, 3, 4
b. 6, 12, 18, 24
c. 6, 10, 14, 18
d. 6, 11, 16, 21

6. Which of the following statements is true?
a. 800 is ten times greater than 8.
b. 3000 is ten times greater than 30.
c. 70 is ten times greater than 700.
d. 900 is ten times greater than 90.

7. Which of the following is the written form for the number 5,320,080?
a. five million, thirty-two thousand, eighty
b. five million, three hundred twenty thousand, eighty
c. five million, three hundred twenty thousand, eight
d. five thousand, three hundred twenty-eight

8. Which of the following is 7,859 rounded to the hundreds place?
a. 7,850
b. 7,860
c. 7,800
d. 7,900

9. Evaluate $452 + 388 =$
a. 740
b. 840
c. 830
d. 930

10. Evaluate $1250 - 487 =$
   a. 837
   b. 737
   c. 763
   d. 863

11. What is the area of the figure to the right?
   a.448 square units
   b.46 square units
   c.92 square units
   d. 348 square units

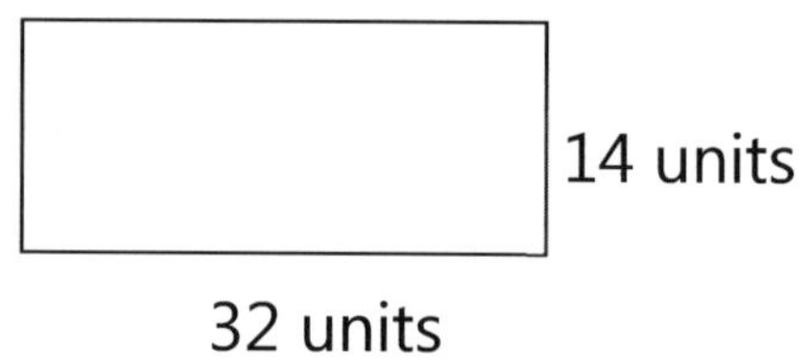

12. Evaluate $457 \times 7 =$
   a. 3199
   b. 2869
   c. 2899
   d. 3189

13. Evaluate $8621 \div 6 =$
   a. 1435 r 5
   b. 1013 r 3
   c. 1535 r 0
   d. 1436 r 5

14. Which fraction model is *not* equivalent to $\frac{3}{5}$?

a. 

b. 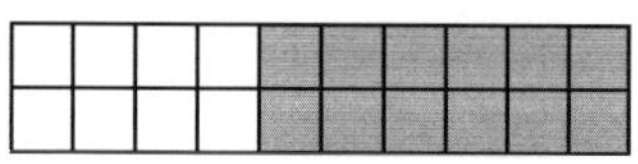

c. 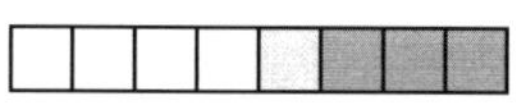

d. 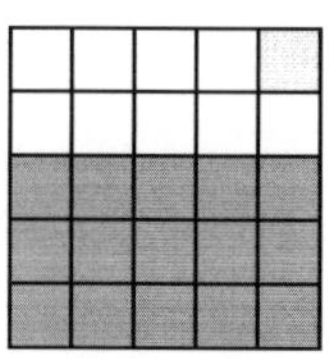

15. Which of the following fractions is equivalent to $\frac{6}{18}$?

a. $\frac{2}{6}$

b. $\frac{2}{3}$

c. $\frac{1}{5}$

d. $\frac{2}{9}$

16. Fill in the blank with the appropriate symbol: $\frac{2}{3}$ ___ $\frac{3}{5}$.

a. >

b. <

c. =

d. Cannot be determined

17. Fill in the blank with the appropriate symbol: $\frac{3}{8}$ ___ $\frac{2}{5}$.

a. >

b. <

c. =

d. Cannot be determined

18. Which equation is represented by the following model?

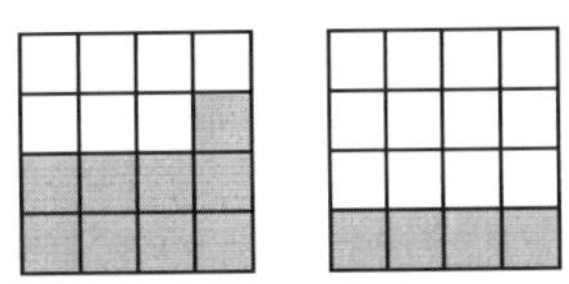

a. $\frac{9}{4}+\frac{4}{4}=\frac{13}{4}$

b. $\frac{7}{16}+\frac{4}{16}=\frac{11}{16}$

c. $\frac{9}{16}+\frac{4}{16}=\frac{13}{16}$

d. $\frac{9}{16}+\frac{12}{16}=\frac{21}{16}$

19. Which of the following expressions is not equal to $\frac{5}{8}$?

a. $\frac{8}{8} - \frac{1}{8} - \frac{1}{8} - \frac{1}{8} - \frac{1}{8}$

b. $\frac{2}{8} + \frac{2}{8} + \frac{1}{8}$

c. $\frac{1}{8} + \frac{1}{8} + \frac{1}{8} + \frac{1}{8} + \frac{1}{8}$

d. $\frac{1}{8} + \frac{2}{8} + \frac{3}{8} + \frac{4}{8} - \frac{5}{8}$

20. Evaluate $4\frac{1}{5} + 3\frac{2}{5} =$

a. $7\frac{3}{10}$

b. $7\frac{3}{5}$

c. $7\frac{1}{5}$

d. $7\frac{2}{5}$

21. Evaluate $11\frac{3}{5} - 8\frac{2}{5} =$

a. $2\frac{4}{5}$

b. $3\frac{4}{5}$

c. $2\frac{1}{5}$

d. $3\frac{1}{5}$

22. Jordan is making a cake. He wants to reduce the amount of sugar in the recipe. If the original recipe calls for $2\frac{1}{3}$ cups of sugar and he wants to decrease it by $\frac{2}{3}$ cup of sugar, how many cups of sugar should Jordan put into the recipe?

a. 1 cup

b. $1\frac{1}{3}$ cups

c. $1\frac{2}{3}$ cups

d. 2 cups

23. A cuckoo clock is being built and the pendulum of the clock needs to be cut from a piece of wood so that it is $\frac{1}{12}$ meter. If you are going to build 5 cuckoo clocks, what will the total length of 5 pendulums be?

a. $\frac{5}{12}$ meter

b. $\frac{1}{60}$ meter

c. $5\frac{1}{12}$ meters

d. $\frac{1}{2}$ meter

24. Evaluate $4 \times \frac{3}{5} =$

a. $\frac{7}{5}$

b. $\frac{3}{20}$

c. $\frac{1}{3}$

d. $\frac{12}{5}$

25. Which equation represents the fraction model shown?

a. $4 \times \frac{4}{5} = \frac{16}{5}$

b. $4 \times \frac{8}{25} = \frac{32}{25}$

c. $4 \times \frac{1}{2} = 2$

d. $4 \times \frac{9}{25} = \frac{36}{25}$

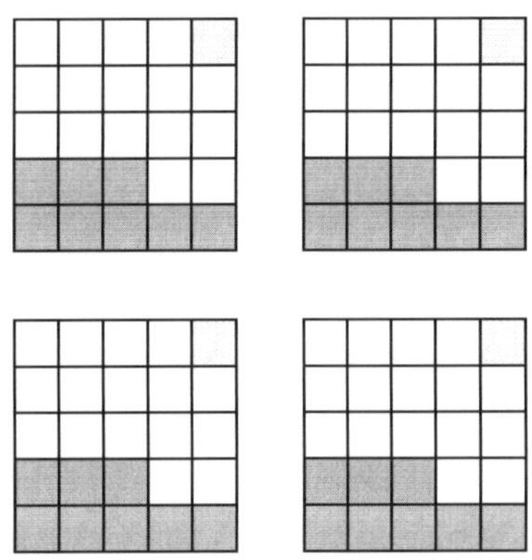

26. While designing a tree fort, you want to have 9 pieces of rope that are $\frac{1}{2}$ meter to make a rope ladder. When you go to the store, how many meters of rope do you ask the clerk to sell you?

a. 4 meters
b. 9 meters
c. $4\frac{1}{2}$ meters
d. 18 meters

27. Add $\frac{7}{10}+\frac{57}{100}$.

a. $\frac{127}{100}$
b. $\frac{62}{100}$
c. $\frac{64}{100}$
d. $\frac{5770}{100}$

28. Rewrite ${}^{45}/_{100}$ as a decimal.

a. 0.45
b. 4.5
c. 0.045
d. 0.0045

29. Fill in the blank with the appropriate symbol to compare the following numbers: 0.24 __ 0.18

a. <
b. >
c. =
d. Cannot be determined

30. You are deciding to go on a long distance bike ride. You ride a total of 3490 meters. Express this in kilometers.

a. 349 kilometers
b. 34900 kilometers
c. 34.90 kilometers
d. 3.490 kilometers

31. While you are working at a certain job, you are paid $40.25 per day. You work 5 days out of the week. You save $20 per week to buy a new bike. How much money do you have left over to spend at the end of the week?

a. $181.25
b. $59.75
c. $101.25
d. $25.25

32. A farmer is making a pen for his pigs. The model of the pen is to the right. What is the perimeter of the pen?

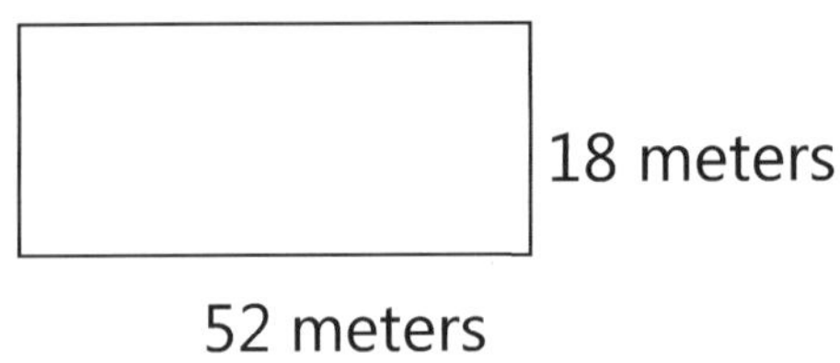

a. 936 meters
b. 70 meters
c. 122 meters
d. 140 meters

33. Richard and Mary are training for a race. On a particular day Richard runs $\frac{5}{8}$ of a mile and Mary runs $\frac{1}{2}$ of a mile. How much further did Richard run than Mary?

a. $\frac{1}{2}$ mile
b. $\frac{2}{3}$ mile
c. $\frac{1}{4}$ mile
d. $\frac{1}{8}$ mile

34. A one-degree angle is $\frac{1}{360}$ of a circle. 180 one-degree angles make up what fraction of a circle?

a. $\frac{1}{4}$

b. $\frac{1}{2}$

c. $\frac{3}{4}$

d. $\frac{4}{5}$

35. What is the measure of $\angle ABC$?

a. 52°

b. 41°

c. 93°

d. Cannot be determined

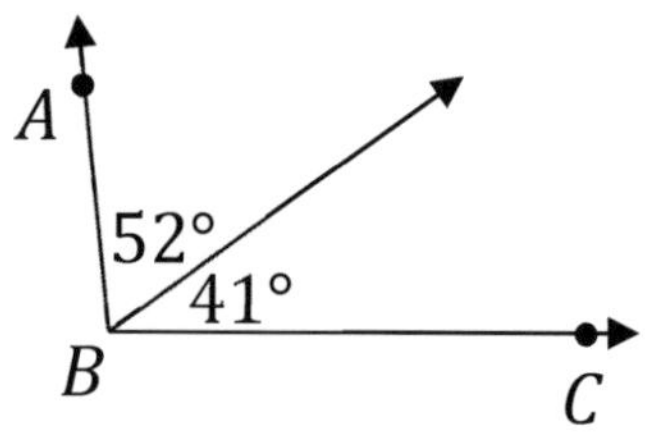

36. Measure the angle using a protractor.

a. 45 °

b. 90°

c. 135°

d. 180°

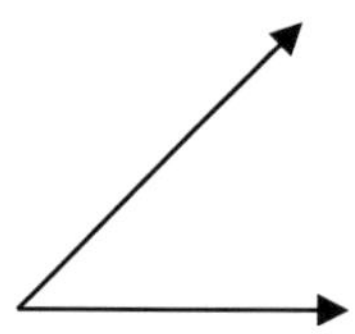

37. If $m\angle ABC = 100°$, what is $m\angle ABD$

a. 82°

b. 122°

c. 88°

d. 78 °

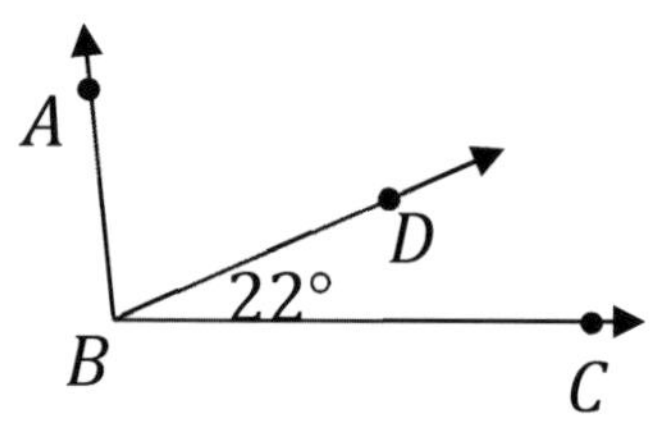

38. Classify the angle based on the measure of the angle.

a. Acute

b. Obtuse

c. Right

d. Straight

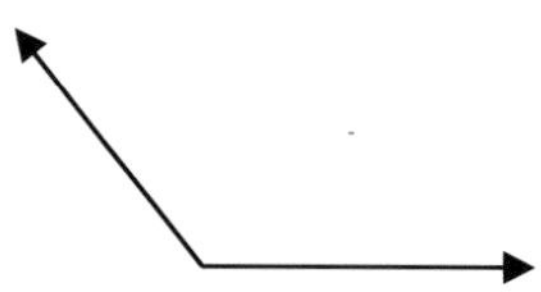

39. Classify the figure.

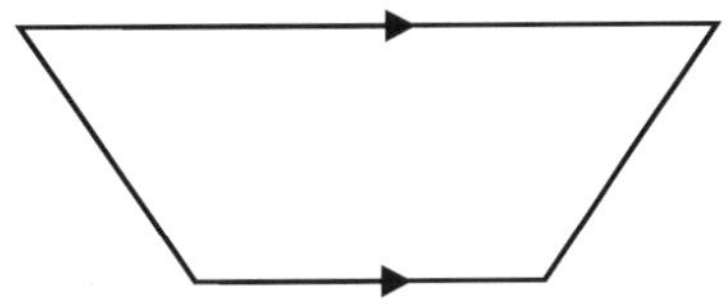

a. Rhombus
b. Trapezoid
c. Kite
d. Pentagon

40.Which of the following shapes do not have line symmetry?

a. 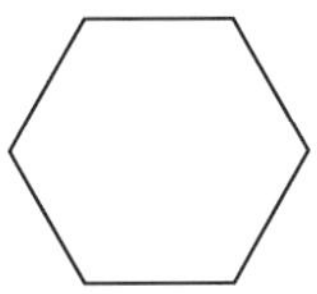

b. 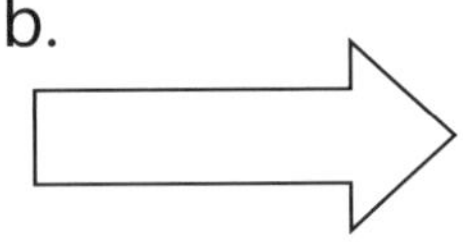

c. 

d. 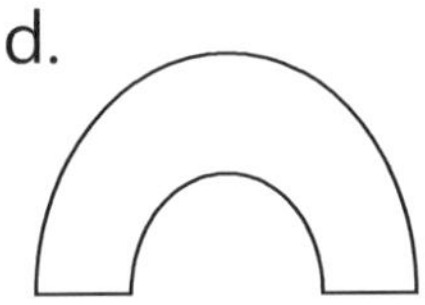

Practice Test #2

Practice Questions

1. Which equation **does not** have the same meaning as *eight times as many as six is forty-eight*?
   a. $8 = 6 \times 48$
   b. $8 \times 6 = 48$
   c. $6 \times 8 = 48$
   d. $48 = 6 \times 8$

2. A weightlifter has only 5-pound weights and placed 14 weights onto the bar he is lifting. How many total pounds did the weightlifter place onto the bar?
   a. 19 pounds
   b. 25 pounds
   c. 50 pounds
   d. 70 pounds

For numbers 3 and 4, use the following information: Lawrence collects aluminum cans for recycling. He collects 8 cans a day and currently has 200 cans.

3. If Lawrence collects cans for 7 days, which equation would you use to determine the number of cans Lawrence has at the end of the 7 days? Use c to represent the total cans in his collection.
   a. $200 \times 7 + 8 = \text{c}$
   b. $8 \times 200 + 7 = \text{c}$
   c. $8 + 7 + 200 = \text{c}$
   d. $8 \times 7 + 200 = c$

4. How many cans will Lawrence have at the end of 7 days?
   a. 215
   b. 256
   c. 1408
   d. 1607

5. Which number listed below is **not** a factor of 72?
   a. 42
   b. 18
   c. 36
   d. 12

6. The numbers 1, 3, 6, 10, and 15 are the start of a set of numbers called 'triangular numbers' because the numbers can be illustrated using a triangle as shown below. Predict the next number in the set.
   a. 20
   b. 21
   c. 22
   d. 23

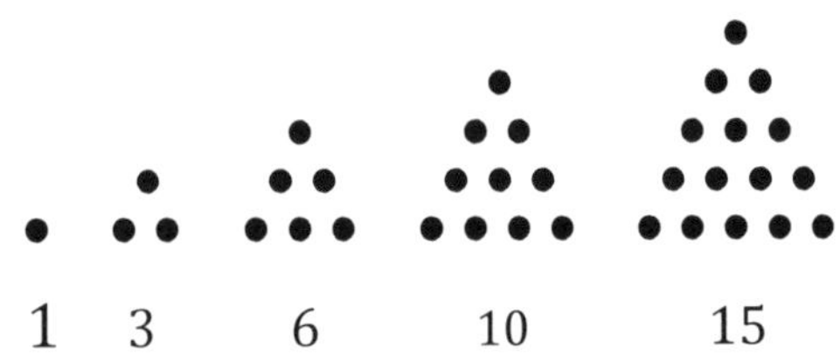

7. How many times greater is 9,000 than 90?
   a. one time greater
   b. ten times greater
   c. one hundred times greater
   d. one thousand times greater

8. What number is represented by *seven hundred forty-five thousand, nine hundred one*?
   a. 745,910
   b. 700,045,901
   c. 745,091
   d. 745,901

9. If 9,512 is rounded to 9,500, what place value was the original number rounded to?

a. thousands place
b. hundreds place
c. tens place
d. ones place

10. Simplify $215 + 796 =$

a. 91011
b.911
c. 1011
d. 1001

11. Simplify $547 - 352 =$

a. 215
b. 115
c. 195
d. 295

12. Simplify $4562 \times 5 =$

a. 22815
b. 22810
c. 203010
d. 102540

13. Simplify $21 \times 47 =$

a. 847
b. 231
c. 987
d. 970

14. The walkway between two large buildings is 1400 square feet. The walkway is 8 feet wide. How long is the walkway?

a. 1392 feet
b. 11200 feet
c. 175 feet
d. 225 feet

15. Which fraction listed below is **not** equivalent to $\frac{15}{20}$?

a. $\frac{20}{25}$
b. $\frac{3}{4}$
c. $\frac{18}{24}$
d. $\frac{30}{40}$

16. Which of the following fractions is greater than $\frac{5}{9}$?

a. $\frac{3}{7}$
b. $\frac{1}{2}$
c. $\frac{2}{3}$
d. None of the above

17. Which statement about the shaded region of the two figures is true?

a. Figure A is greater than Figure B
b. Figure A is less than Figure B
c. Figure A is equal to figure B
d. No comparison can be made

Figure A

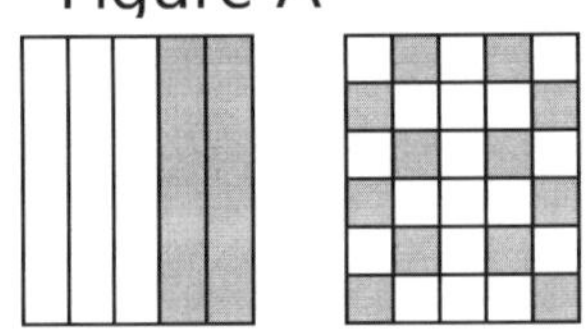

18. If you changed 3 of the shaded portions from the figure below to non-shaded, what fraction of the figure will be shaded?

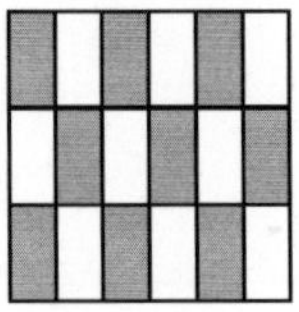

a. $\frac{1}{2}$

b. $\frac{8}{15}$

c. $\frac{2}{3}$

d. $\frac{1}{3}$

19. Which of the following expressions is equal to $\frac{7}{10}$?

a. $\frac{2}{10}+\frac{2}{10}+\frac{2}{10}+\frac{1}{10}$

b. $\frac{1}{10}+\frac{1}{10}+\frac{1}{10}+\frac{5}{10}$

c. $\frac{1}{10}+\frac{2}{10}+\frac{3}{10}$

d. $\frac{1}{8}+\frac{2}{8}+\frac{2}{8}+\frac{2}{8}$

20. Simplify $2\frac{4}{5}+3\frac{2}{5}=$

a. $5\frac{3}{5}$

b. $5\frac{7}{5}$

c. $6\frac{3}{5}$

d. $6\frac{1}{5}$

21. Simplify $4\frac{1}{3}-2\frac{2}{3}=$

a. $2\frac{1}{3}$

b. $2\frac{3}{6}$

c. $1\frac{1}{9}$

d. $1\frac{2}{3}$

22. Rebecca is cutting wood slats to make a chair. She has a board $10\frac{2}{3}$ feet in length and needs to cut $5\frac{1}{3}$ feet from the board. How long will the remaining board be after she makes the cut?

a. 16 feet

b. $5\frac{2}{3}$ feet

c. $5\frac{1}{3}$ feet

d. 5 feet

23. Which equation below is true?

a. $3 \times \frac{1}{5} = \frac{3}{15}$

b. $4 \times \frac{2}{3} = \frac{2}{12}$

c. $5 \times \frac{6}{7} = \frac{11}{7}$

d. $6 \times \frac{2}{5} = \frac{12}{5}$

24. Which of the following is equal to half of $\frac{15}{24}$?

a. $\frac{15}{12}$

b. 5

c. $\frac{5}{8}$

d. $\frac{5}{16}$

25. A recipe for cookies calls for $\frac{9}{4}$ cups of sugar. Miguel wants to triple the recipe. How many cups of sugar should Miguel use to make the cookies?

a. $\frac{27}{4}$ cups
b. $\frac{9}{12}$ cups
c. $\frac{27}{12}$ cups
d. 3 cups

26. Which of the following expressions add up to $^{47}/_{100}$?

a. $\frac{40}{100}+\frac{7}{10}$
b. $\frac{70}{100}+\frac{4}{100}$
c. $\frac{70}{10}+\frac{4}{100}$
d. $\frac{4}{10}+\frac{7}{100}$

27. Rewrite $\frac{3}{10}$ as a decimal.

a. 0.03
b. 3.0
c. 0.003
d. 0.3

28. Fill in the blank with the appropriate symbol: 0.742 ________ 0.745

a. >
b. <
c. =
d. Cannot be determined

29. 6 hours is equivalent to how many minutes?
   a. 240 minutes
   b. 300 minutes
   c. 360 minutes
   d. 21600 minutes

30. You need to measure a flag pole that is 4 meters tall. How many centimeters tall is the flag pole?
   a. 40 centimeters
   b. 400 centimeters
   c. 4000 centimeters
   d. Cannot be determined

31. On Monday, Joan ran 3.2 miles, on Tuesday she ran 1.5 miles, and on Wednesday she ran 4.6 miles. How many miles did she run over the course of the three days?
   a. 9.3 miles
   b. 8.3 miles
   c. 8.6 miles
   d. 9.6 miles

32. Melanie and Steve are buying new carpet for their bedroom. The dimensions of their bedroom are 12 feet by 14 feet. What is the area of the carpet they need to buy to fit their bedroom?
   a. 168 square feet
   b. 144 square feet
   c. 196 square feet
   d. 52 square feet

33.How much longer is line A than line B?
   a. 2 units
   b. 3 units
   c. $2\frac{1}{2}$ units
   d. $1\frac{1}{2}$ units

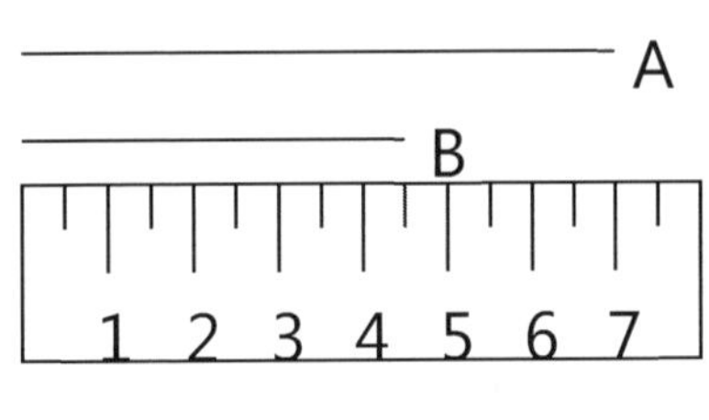

34. A one-degree angle is $\frac{1}{360}$ of a circle. 36 one-degree angles make up what fraction of a circle?

a. $\frac{1}{36}$
b. $\frac{1}{2}$
c. $\frac{1}{10}$
d. $\frac{1}{5}$

35. $\angle A$ consists of 15 one-degree angles. What is the angle measure of $\angle A$?

a. 10°
b. 15°
c. 20°
d. Cannot be determined

36. Use a protractor to measure the degrees of the angle.

a. 20°
b. 45°
c. 75°
d. 90°

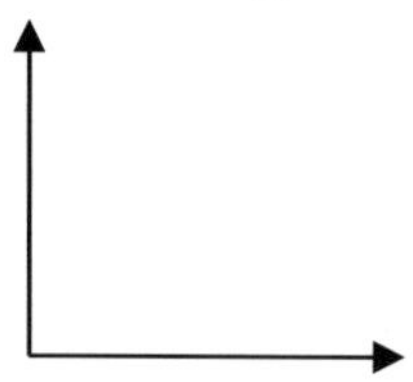

37. What is the measure of $\angle ABC$?

a. 40°
b. 1400°
c. 140°
d. 450°

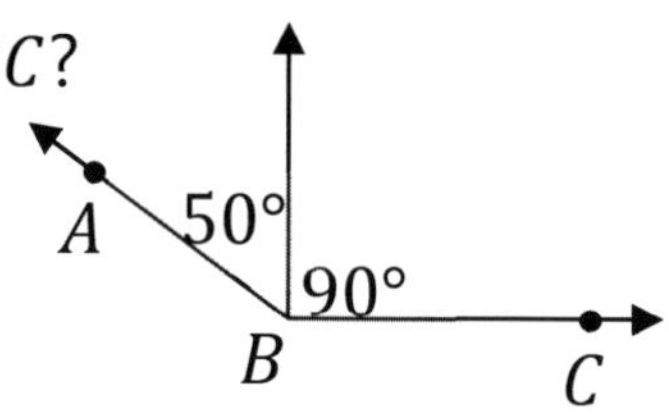

38. Classify the figure.

a. Ray EG
b. Line EG
c. Angle EG
d. Line Segment EG

39. Classify the figure.

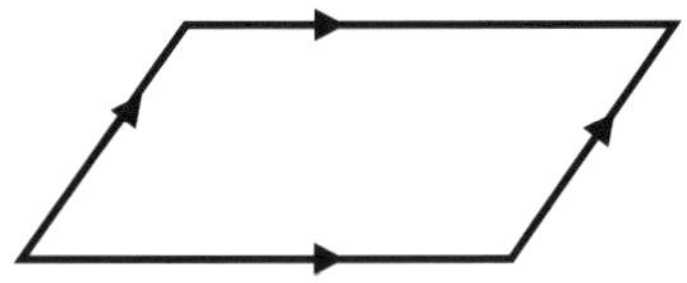

a. Parallelogram
b. Square
c. Rectangle
d. Rhombus

40. Which line is a line of symmetry for the figure?

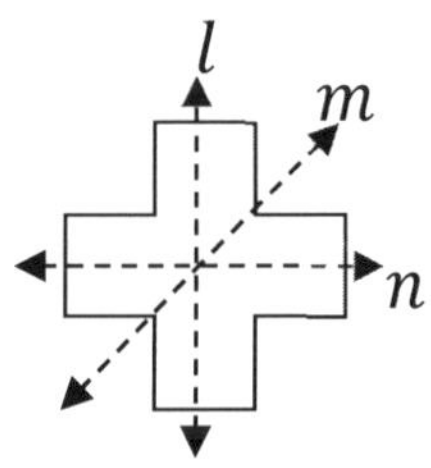

a. Line l
b. Line m
c. Line n
d. All of the above

Thank You

We at Mometrix would like to extend our heartfelt thanks to you, our friend and patron, for allowing us to play a part in your journey. It is a privilege to serve people from all walks of life who are unified in their commitment to building the best future they can for themselves.

The preparation you devote to these important testing milestones may be the most valuable educational opportunity you have for making a real difference in your life. We encourage you to put your heart into it—that feeling of succeeding, overcoming, and yes, conquering will be well worth the hours you've invested.

We want to hear your story, your struggles and your successes, and if you see any opportunities for us to improve our materials so we can help others even more effectively in the future, please share that with us as well. **The team at Mometrix would be absolutely thrilled to hear from you!** So please, send us an email (support@mometrix.com) and let's stay in touch.

Online Resources

Due to our efforts to try to keep this book to a manageable length, we've created a link that will give you access to all of your online resources:

mometrix.com/resources719/ssmcag4mathwb

It's Your Moment, Let's Celebrate It!

Share your story @mometrixtestpreparation